THE MARTINI BOOK

THE MARTINI BOOK

201 WAYS TO MIX THE PERFECT AMERICAN COCKTAIL

SALLY ANN BERK

Photographs by
ZEVA OELBAUM

BLACK DOG
& LEVENTHAL
PUBLISHERS

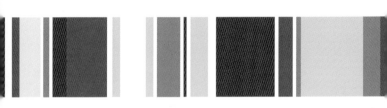

The Martini Book

Copyright © 1997, 2007 Black Dog & Leventhal Publishers, Inc.

Published by
Black Dog & Leventhal Publishers, Inc.
151 West 19th Street
New York, NY 10011

Distributed by
Workman Publishing Company
225 Varick Street
New York, NY 10014

Printed in China
Contributor: Kylie Foxx
Designer: Andy Taray / Ohioboy.com

ISBN-10: 1-57912-716-9
ISBN-13: 978-1-57912-716-9

h g f e d c b a

Library of Congress Cataloging-in-Publication Data is on file at
Black Dog & Leventhal Publishers, Inc.

THE MARTINI BOOK

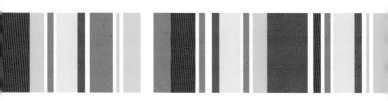

CONTENTS

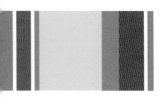 "A well-made martini ... correctly chilled and nicely served, has been more often my true friend than any two-legged creature."

—M.F.K. FISHER

INTRODUCTION:
THE MARTINI

Icy cold, clear, and quintessentially American, the martini has come to stand for sophistication and elegance, luxury spiked with a dash of daring. Born and bred in the United States, it is now famous the world over, its renown bolstered in no small part by the devotion of well-known characters both fictional and factual. Sometimes called a "silver bullet," the martini is clean and smooth, and always hits its mark.

Presidents and movie stars, journalists and poets, fictional characters and their creators have all looked to the martini for inspiration. No other cocktail engenders the kind of passion true martini purists exhibit when mixing or defending their unique take on the drink. And no other cocktail has such a complicated folklore.

The origin of the martini has been the subject of much debate. It was invented sometime during the latter part of the nineteenth century, but beyond that one probable fact, the stories of its origin diverge. One theory places the martini in the San Francisco Bay area after the Gold Rush. Another places it, again during the Gold Rush era, in Martinez, California, thus the name. Still another theory credits the bartender at the Hoffman House in New York around 1880. A fourth story attributes the martini to an Italian immigrant named Martini di Arma di Taggia, who tended bar at

the Knickerbocker Hotel in New York in the early part of the twentieth century. And yet another tale claims the martini was first conceived in the Netherlands.

There is no doubt that *gin* was developed in the Netherlands, but not the martini. Too much evidence points to America as its birthplace. New Yorkers usually adhere to the Hoffman House theory, while West Coasters prefer the San Francisco theory—everyone wants to lay claim to this iconic cocktail.

But why and how did this drink become a cultural icon? Why not the Rob Roy? The Rusty Nail? The Manhattan?

All of these drinks have their place among the pantheon of classic cocktails, but the martini has long been the favorite of jet-setters, politicians, rainmakers, and other high-profile people. From this prime position it has captured the fancy and the taste of the general public, and—except for a lapse during the 1970s—the martini has remained the quintessential cocktail ever since.

Perhaps the classic martini owes its status to its simplicity—the blessed marriage of cold gin and vermouth, accompanied by nothing more than a Spanish olive and a cocktail napkin. Or perhaps the contemporary martini is popular because of its versatility—today the cocktail is a model of constant creation and reinvention. Beginning first with the vodka martini, which quickly gathered a zealous following, the cocktail canon now includes a multitude of sweet and savory 'tinis, some laced with fruit or herb essences, others with cloudy olive brine or decadent liqueurs. But maybe it's just that creating a martini is almost alchemic: from some basic elements, one can create gold—or the cocktail equivalent.

☐ | Did You Know?

Sweet vermouth, or rosso, is a reddish vermouth used in Manhattans. Early recipes for martinis also used sweet vermouth.

SETTING UP YOUR MARTINI BAR

A martini is one of life's little pleasures, as much to sip and savor as to shake (or stir) and pour. To set up your own martini bar, you need only some simple ingredients and some essential, but readily available, equipment. (If you plan to make some of the more inventive martinis in this book—and we think you should—you can purchase the additional ingredients as needed; you will most likely have any additional equipment called for in your kitchen already.)

Y | Did You Know?

It is widely believed that one of contenders for the "original" martini, the Martinez Cocktail, was created with Old Tom gin.

INGREDIENTS

For a classic silver bullet martini, you simply need to choose your poison—gin or vodka—and add dry vermouth and olives. For the more complex concoctions, you'll want to stock up on flavored vodkas, juices, garnishes, and liqueurs. Here's a rundown of the basics and not so basics.

SPIRITS

Gin comes to us from the Netherlands, where it was called *genievre,* which means "juniper." It is a clear liquor, distilled from grain and flavored with juniper berries.

There are three kinds of gin available today—Genever, Old Tom, and London Dry. Genever is the original Dutch formula. It is a highly flavored gin and is not usually used in martinis. Old Tom, a nondry gin, is created when barley malt or sweetener is added to dry gin. It is not readily available, but its cousin, Pimm's Cup, is still served as a cocktail.

The gin most people know is London Dry. This is the gin served in bars and found in liquor stores the world over. All spirits are distilled once, but the craft of gin making is exemplified during the second distillation. A gin smith creates a fine dry gin in the redistillation of the liquor. During this second distillation, flavorings are added. It is not unusual to find citrus peels, herbs, and spices added during the second distillation. Without them, gin— deliciously, delicately fruity, and herbaceous—would not exist.

The Secret Life of Gin

Popular myth holds that gin was first invented as a blood cleanser by a seventeenth-century chemist. After its invention, the flavorful liquor's popularity grew throughout Europe and spread to the Colonies. Dickens wrote about gin shops and Hogarth painted them. Henry Hudson brought it with him on his expeditions to the New World. Gin was easy to make because it required no aging. This is why gin became immensely popular during Prohibition—you could distill it anywhere.

While one can use almost any kind of vodka, high quality or poor, to make a good vodka martini, the quality, taste, and smoothness of different gins can make or break the drink. Gin is very easy to manufacture, which means that you really get what you pay for; some gins are excellent, and others would do better as paint thinners. You should invest in the very best gin you can afford.

Although quality, or "premium," gins vary greatly in flavor and smoothness, there really is no absolute "best"—it's all a matter of personal preference. To figure out which gin(s) to purchase, we recommend bellying up to your favorite bar and tasting a few to see which you like. Some suggestions:

- **BEEFEATER**

- **BOMBAY**

- **BOMBAY SAPPHIRE**

- **GORDON'S**

- **HENDRICKS**

- **KENSINGTON**

- **OLD RAJ**

- **TANQUERAY**

Vodka is a Russian word meaning "little water." It has its origins in Russia but is produced worldwide. It was originally made from distilling potatoes, but can be, and is, made from any grain. It is a neutral spirit, which means it must be flavorless by law. It is not aged.

Many purists consider the vodka martini a bastardization of a fine drink. Others consider it a legitimate variation and believe it has its rightful place in the martini pantheon. Even though vodka martinis did not become popular until the 1960s, vodka is an essential ingredient in the martini popularized by James Bond, and many of the new martini incarnations (a large number of which you'll find in this book) cannot be made without it.

Many people will argue that more expensive vodka tastes better or is smoother. However, vodka shouldn't have a flavor to begin with unless it is flavored vodka. The only way to resolve this argument is to buy a bottle of bargain vodka and a bottle of premium vodka, remove the labels, and chill them to near freezing. Sip one, then the other, and see if you can tell the difference. Some people will argue that you can't, but of course, others will tell you that Ketel One is better than Stoli, and Grey Goose is the best. In the end, it's up to you.

As with gin, when you invest in a vodka, use your personal preferences for flavor (if you can detect one), burn (the sensation the vodka leaves in your mouth and throat), and texture (Is it smooth? Slightly oily? Which do you prefer?). Some high-quality options include:

- **ABSOLUT (DISTILLED FROM WHEAT)**

- **ARMADALE (DISTILLED FROM WHEAT AND BARLEY)**

- **BELVEDERE (DISTILLED FROM RYE)**

- **CHOPIN (DISTILLED FROM POTATOES)**

- **CÎROC (DISTILLED FROM GRAPES)**

- **GREY GOOSE (DISTILLED FROM WHEAT, BARLEY, AND RYE)**

- **KETEL ONE (DISTILLED FROM WHEAT)**

- **SMIRNOFF (DISTILLED FROM GRAINS)**

- **STOLICHNAYA (DISTILLED FROM WHEAT)**

- **ZYR (DISTILLED FROM WHEAT AND RYE)**

Flavored vodkas have become increasingly popular in the past twenty years or so—both in the more elaborate 'tinis that feature them, as well as straight up or splashed with soda. The modern martini mixer makes use of everything from commercial citrus-flavored vodkas to homemade flavored vodkas spiked with coffee beans or hot peppers. You should include as many flavored vodkas as possible when creating your martini bar. If you don't find one you need, you can always make your own. (The best pepper vodka is homemade.) Simply take the flavoring you desire—a hot pepper, say, or a vanilla bean—and soak it in a bottle of plain vodka for at least a week. Taste the vodka. If it needs more oomph, soak the flavoring for a few more days. When the vodka is flavored the way you want it, strain it into a clean bottle.

Some commercially made (or homemade) flavors to consider include cranberry, currant, lemon, orange, peach, pepper, raspberry, strawberry, and vanilla.

Flavored gin is available from some distillers, but we don't recommend it—gin is flavorful enough as it is. A number of recipes in this book also call for **scotch**, **whiskey**, and **rum**, and any good home bar will include these other spirits on its shelves. Remember, quality counts. Be sure to spring for the finest you can afford.

The Deep Freeze

Gin or vodka, a splash of vermouth or none—there's one thing all martinis must be, and that's cold. Whether you prefer your martini unadulterated or infused with a multitude of flavors, you'll want it to be as cold as possible.

Some bartenders recommend shaking or stirring the cocktail over ice until the shaker is frigid and glistening with frost; others say that the liquor must be chilled for at least six hours (or given a permanent home in the freezer) to ensure the perfect temperature (and to obviate the need for ice, which can dilute the liquor). Choose whichever method you wish—just make sure that martini is chilly.

Stir It Up

Simple syrup is indeed simple to make: combine two parts granulated sugar with one part boiling water, stirring until the sugar dissolves completely. Bottle the concoction, and keep it on hand to sweeten any variety of drinks, from martinis to iced tea.

Vermouth is a key ingredient in the classic martinis, whether vodka or gin based. It is a fortified wine that has been flavored with various herbs and spices.

The word "vermouth" comes from the German word *wermut,* which means "wormwood." Before wormwood was discovered to be poisonous, it was used in making vermouth (and its notorious relative, absinthe). The martini is made with white dry vermouth, also known as French vermouth, a white liquid that can also be drunk as a cocktail. This should not be confused with bianco, an Italian version, which is also white but much sweeter.

Even though a dry martini uses practically no vermouth, it should be included. We recommend Martini Extra Dry (considered the "original" vermouth), which is made in Italy, or Noilly Prat from France.

MIXERS

Mixers, for a martini? Well, for the classic silver bullet you'd want nothing more than some very dry vermouth (see above)—and even that might be too much of a dilution. But for the sweet and sassy cocktails that turn the whole concept of the martini on its head, you'll want to have some juices, liqueurs, and other mixers on hand (you may need to purchase additional items depending on the drinks you're mixing):

JUICE: apple, cranberry, grapefruit, orange, pineapple, pome-granate, Rose's lime juice

LIQUEURS: amaretto, Angostura or orange bitters, chocolate liqueur, coffee liqueur, crème de cassis, curaçao, triple sec, schnapps (apple, berry, cinnamon, peach, sour apple, sour berry, sour cherry), Irish cream, Frangelico

SYRUPS: chocolate, ginger, honey, lychee, simple (see Stir It Up, p. 22)

GARNISHES

The quintessential garnish for a martini is a Spanish olive—a small green olive, sometimes stuffed with a pimento. (The less commonly used black olive makes it a Buckeye Martini.) But just as there are many martini options—pure and clean, fresh and fruity, green and herbaceous—so there are a great many garnishes to choose from. Give one of the following a go, or follow a whim of your own—if you think something might taste good with your martini, by all means, drop it in or prop it on the glass:

- ASPARAGUS SPEARS

- BLACK CHERRIES ON THE STEM

- CANDIED GINGER

- CANDY CANES

- CHIVES

- CHOCOLATE OR WHITE CHOCOLATE CURLS OR KISSES

- CINNAMON STICKS

- CITRUS TWISTS OR PEELS

- COCKTAIL ONIONS

- COCOA POWDER; SUPERFINE SUGAR; CINNAMON SUGAR OR VANILLA SUGAR; COARSE SALT; ICED TEA, LEMONADE, OR FRUIT PUNCH DRINK MIX (FOR THE OUTER RIM OF THE GLASS)

- FRESH BERRIES (IN THE GLASS)

- FRESH FRUIT SLICES (BANANA, STRAWBERRY, PINEAPPLE, APPLE, PEAR, KIWI, ETC.)

- FRESH HERB SPRIGS

- FRESH ORGANIC BLOSSOMS

- GUM DROPS

- JALAPEÑO SLICES (FRESH OR PICKLED)

- JAPANESE "JUICY" GUMMY CANDIES

- OLIVES
  ALMOND-STUFFED OLIVES
  BLACK OLIVES
  BLUE CHEESE-STUFFED OLIVES
  CALAMATA OLIVES
  GARLIC-STUFFED OLIVES
  HERB-STUFFED OLIVES
  PIMENTO-STUFFED GREEN OLIVES
  WASABI-STUFFED OLIVES

- PICKLED CHERRY TOMATO

- PICKLED PLUM (UMEBOSHI)

- POMEGRANATE SEEDS (IN THE GLASS)

- RED HOT CANDIES (IN THE GLASS)

- ROCK CANDY ON A STICK

- STAR ANISE PODS

- SUGARED FLOWERS

- SWEDISH FISH

- VANILLA BEANS

- VEGETABLES
  (SLICES OF FRESH BEET, CARROT, CUCUMBER, HEIRLOOM TOMATO, ZUCCHINI)

To your h

	Martini	Daiquiri	Ba
	ADD OLIVE	JUICE OF 1/2 LIME	
	1 OZ. FRENCH VERMOUTH	1 TEASPOON SUGAR	
	2 OZ. GIN	1/2 OZ. LIGHT RUM	
	STIR WITH ICE	SHAKE WITH FINE ICE	
	TWIST OF LEMON PEEL	COCKTAIL GLASS	

Martini—The Drink of Presidents and Publicists

Since its invention, the martini has been the preferred cocktail of presidents and heads of state. FDR even carried a martini kit on international summits, and Gerald Ford thought the martini the exemplar of civilized life. Prize-winning writers have sung its praise, allowing themselves one (E.B. White) or several (William Faulkner) for fortification when facing the empty page.

Certainly not the sole territory of powerful men, Dorothy Parker enjoyed martinis as did and do many professional women.

Today the martini exemplifies both sophistication and celebration—it is the preferred cocktail of many professionals and is increasingly popular with the well-heeled nighttime bar crowd.

On the martini shaker glass:

MARTINI
2/3 DRY GIN
1/3 FRENCH VERMOUTH
DASH ORANGE BITTERS
STIR WITH CRACKED ICE
SERVE WITH OLIVE

DAIQUIRI
1-1/2 JIGGER CUBAN RUM
JUICE OF 1 LIME
1/2 TSP. POWDER SUGAR
SHAKE WELL WITH ICE
STRAIN AND SERVE

BRONX
1/2 DRY GIN
1/4 FRENCH VERMOUTH
1/6 ITALIAN VERMOUTH
1/6 ORANGE JUICE
SHAKE WITH ICE. STRAIN

On the left glass:

...n Collins
JUICE OF 1
ME or LEMON
TEASPOON
SUGAR
2 OZ
GIN
SHAKE AND
ADD ICE
TOP SODA
AND FRUIT

EQUIPMENT
SHAKERS

You will need a good stainless steel cocktail shaker with a strainer and a lid. Stainless steel will chill a drink quickly and uniformly (and won't react with the ingredients in your drink, as other metals can). For those who prefer their martini stirred, not shaken, a good mixing glass and a long stainless steel stirring spoon are essential. Cocktail shakers and mixing glasses come in many designs and sizes. You can find anything from deco to modern or postmodern if you look hard enough. Choose a shaker and mixing glass that complement your glassware.

GLASSES

Be sure to have at least eight martini, or cocktail, glasses on hand.
These iconic triangle-shaped glasses—sex symbols coyly perched
on a bare leg—not only epitomize the drink, but dress up any casual
cocktail. They are made of glass and can be found in good glassware or home furnishing stores. The finer the crystal, the greater
the martini experience. Never use plastic! And you should also
keep some crystal highball glasses handy for those who prefer to
drink their martinis on the rocks.

Movers and Shakers

Ever since the birth of the cocktail, professional and home bartenders have used cocktail shakers not only to make drinks, but to make fashion statements. They add a touch of class.

Shakers have always reflected the design sensibilities of the era in which they're used. In many design museums you can find gorgeous Art Deco shakers from the '20s and '30s. These accoutrements served as conversation pieces as well as utilitarian items.

During the Great Depression of the 1930s, elegant barware was an affordable luxury for a "have not" era. These gorgeous utensils not only made bartending an art, they deflected from the dingy realities of the time. Perhaps one could not travel to Paris, but one could recreate the elegant atmosphere of the Ritz with the right shaker and glass. And one could call to mind the elegance of a black tie evening with a novelty penguin cocktail shaker.

After World War II and into the '50s, as we entered the atomic age, barware began to look like rocket ships. Cocktail shakers were decorated with pictures of the atom and shaped like missiles.

Early shakers were made of glass, silver plate, silver, Bakelite, and chromium. But since the 1960s, most shakers have been made of stainless steel—a durable, nonreactive material that chills the cocktail completely.

Brand-new shakers are available at houseware and department stores in a range of prices and styles; or go for a vintage or antique barware set (just be careful with glass, and be sure to avoid acidic ingredients with any metals other than stainless steel). If you shop at flea markets for your set, you can start a collection for very little money, and you'll have some usable art to display as you shake up martinis for your friends.

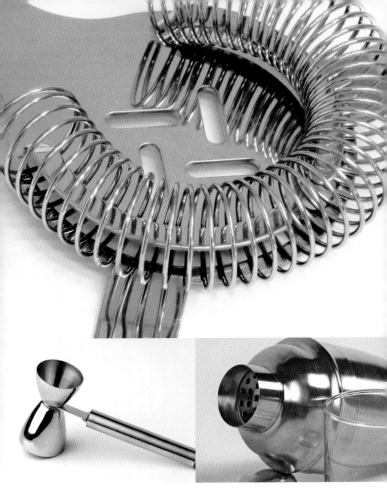

GADGETS AND OTHER GOODIES

There are several gadgets available to the martini mixer; they really aren't necessary, but they are fun. Eye droppers and misters for vermouth assure the very driest martini, and there's even something called a "martini tester," which allegedly checks the vermouth content of a martini.

As for tools, all you need are some basics: stainless steel measuring spoons, bar spoons, a double-sided jigger measure (usually a "jigger"—1½ ounces—on one end, and a "pony"—1 ounce—on the other), and a sharp paring knife for cutting garnishes and making citrus peel and zest. You'll also want some toothpicks or skewers for creating elaborate garnishes and maybe some swizzle sticks—simple, sophisticated, or outrageous. Finally, keep on hand some clean bar towels and coasters or bar napkins (martini glasses are beautiful, but notoriously difficult to handle without sloshing their contents).

Y | Did You Know?

The quality of the water used to make ice greatly affects the quality of a cocktail. Even if you are shaking and straining a drink, the ice should be made of pure spring or distilled water. Keep plenty on hand to make your ice.

THE
CLASSICS

MARTINI ➳

6 parts gin

1 part dry vermouth

Cocktail olive

Combine liquid ingredients in a mixing glass with ice cubes and stir well. Strain into a chilled cocktail glass and garnish with olive.

MARTINIS FOR FOUR

1 cup gin

1 tablespoon dry vermouth

4 large pimento-stuffed green olives

Fill a 4-cup glass measuring cup ⅓ full with ice. Add gin and vermouth and stir gently. Immediately strain mixture into chilled martini glasses. Add an olive to each glass and serve immediately.

VODKA MARTINI ➳

6 parts vodka

2 parts dry vermouth (or to taste)

Olive

Combine liquid ingredients in a cocktail shaker with cracked ice and shake well. Strain into a chilled cocktail glass and garnish with olive.

"Anyone can write books,
but it takes an artist to
make a dry martini."
—NOEL COWARD

MARTINIS
WITH
A TWIST

Measure for Measure

You'll see a number of different measurements called for in the recipes throughout this book. Here's a little cheat sheet to help you decipher the bar-speak and convert from one type of measurement to another. (Please note that when a recipe calls for parts [as in, "6 parts gin, 1 part vermouth"] simply measure out the liquids in any equal amount, using the ratio shown. In the previous example, if you chose a pony to equal a part, you would pour out 6 ponies of gin and 1 pony of vermouth.)

DASH:	¹⁄₃₂ ounce, ⅓ teaspoon, about 10 drops
CUP:	8 ounces, 16 tablespoons
JIGGER:	1½ ounces, approximately 1 shot, 45 ml.
PONY:	1 ounce, 6 teaspoons, 2 tablespoons, 30 ml.
PINCH:	about ⅛ teaspoon
SPLASH:	¼ ounce, 1½ teaspoons
TABLESPOON:	about ⅜ ounce
TEASPOON:	about ⅛ ounce

☂ | Did You Know?

Ernest Hemingway was a correspondent during World War II and covered the liberation of Paris. He also personally saw to the "liberation" of the Ritz in the Place Vendome. After the Allies had liberated the city, Hemingway and a group of journalist friends went to the Ritz. The hotel was not damaged, but it was empty except for the manager, who welcomed them and put them into rooms. When asked what they needed, Hemingway ordered fifty martinis.

ABSOLUTE MARTINI

5 parts vodka

1 part triple sec

2 parts fresh lemon juice

1 dash orange bitters

Combine all ingredients in a cocktail shaker with cracked ice and shake well. Strain into a chilled cocktail glass.

ALLEN COCKTAIL ◄

4 parts gin

1 part maraschino liqueur

½ teaspoon fresh lemon juice

Lemon twist

Combine liquid ingredients in a cocktail shaker with cracked ice and shake well. Strain into a chilled cocktail glass and garnish with lemon twist.

ALLIES COCKTAIL

3 parts gin

2 parts dry vermouth

1 teaspoon Jagermeister

Combine all ingredients in a cocktail shaker with cracked ice and stir. Strain into a chilled cocktail glass.

ALTERNATINI

6 parts vodka

½ teaspoon sweet vermouth

½ teaspoon dry vermouth

1 teaspoon white crème de cacao

Sweetened cocoa powder

Hershey's kiss

Rim a chilled cocktail glass with sweetened cocoa powder. Combine liquid ingredients in a cocktail shaker with cracked ice and shake well. Strain into cocktail glass and garnish with Hershey's kiss.

APERITIVO

6 parts gin

3 parts white Sambuca

3 to 5 dashes orange bitters

Orange peel

Combine liquid ingredients in a mixing glass with ice cubes and stir. Strain into a chilled cocktail glass and garnish with orange peel.

APPLE PIE MARTINI ⚓

6 parts vanilla-flavored vodka

1 part Calvados

1 part dry vermouth

Apple slice

Combine liquid ingredients in a cocktail shaker with cracked ice and shake well. Strain into a chilled cocktail glass and garnish with a thin slice of apple.

ARMADA MARTINI

6 parts vodka

2 parts amontillado sherry

Orange twist

Combine liquid ingredients in a mixing glass with cracked ice and stir. Strain into a chilled cocktail glass and garnish with orange twist.

ARTILLERY COCKTAIL

6 parts gin

2 parts sweet vermouth

Combine ingredients in a cocktail shaker with cracked ice and shake well. Strain into a chilled cocktail glass.

AU COURANT BLACK CURRANTINI

3 ounces currant-flavored vodka

½ teaspoon fino sherry or dry cocktail sherry

½ teaspoon crème de cassis

Slice of lemon

Combine liquid ingredients in a cocktail shaker with cracked ice and stir well. Strain into a chilled cocktail glass and garnish with lemon slice.

BABYFACE MARTINI

6 parts strawberry-flavored vodka

1 part dry vermouth

½ teaspoon maraschino liqueur

Fresh strawberry

Combine liquid ingredients in a cocktail shaker with cracked ice and shake well. Strain into a chilled cocktail glass and garnish with strawberry.

Who Said It?

"I've got to get out of these wet clothes and into a dry martini." This immortal line has been attributed to Robert Benchley, Billy Wilder, and Alexander Woollcott. No one is sure who actually said it. All three men were known for their bons mots. Our money's on Woollcott, drama critic for the *New York Times* during the 1920s and 1930s. He also appeared in several screwball comedies. It is believed he uttered this line after shooting a scene where he was tossed into a swimming pool, fully clothed.

BARBED WIRE

6 parts vodka

1 teaspoon sweet vermouth

½ teaspoon Pernod

½ teaspoon Chambord

Lemon twist

Combine liquid ingredients in a cocktail shaker with cracked ice and shake well. Strain into a chilled cocktail glass and garnish with lemon twist.

BARNUM

6 parts gin

1 part apricot brandy

3 to 5 dashes Angostura bitters

3 to 5 dashes lemon juice

Combine all ingredients in a cocktail shaker with cracked ice and shake well. Strain into a chilled cocktail glass.

BEADLESTONE

6 parts scotch

3 parts dry vermouth

Combine ingredients in a mixing glass with ice cubes and stir well. Strain into a chilled cocktail glass.

BENNETT

6 parts gin

½ teaspoon bar sugar

3 to 5 dashes Angostura bitters

Combine all ingredients in a cocktail shaker with cracked ice and shake well. Strain into a chilled cocktail glass.

BERRYTINI

6 parts currant vodka

1 part raspberry eau-de-vie

Fresh raspberries

Combine liquid ingredients in a cocktail shaker with cracked ice and shake well. Strain into a chilled cocktail glass and garnish with raspberries.

BLACK AND WHITE MARTINI ➻

6 parts vanilla vodka

2 parts crème de cacao

Black and white licorice candies

Combine liquid ingredients in a cocktail shaker with cracked ice and shake well. Strain into a chilled cocktail glass and garnish with black and white licorice candies.

"One drink is alright, two is too
many, three is not enough."
—JAMES THURBER

BLACK DOG

6 parts light rum

1 part dry vermouth

Pitted black olive

Combine liquid ingredients in mixing glass with cracked ice and stir well. Strain into a chilled cocktail glass and garnish with olive.

BLOODHOUND

6 parts gin

2 parts sweet vermouth

2 parts dry vermouth

3 fresh strawberries, hulled

Fresh strawberry for garnish

Combine all ingredients in a blender and mix until well blended. Pour into a chilled cocktail glass and garnish with fresh strawberry.

BLUE MOON MARTINI

6 parts gin

1 part blue curaçao

Lemon twist

Combine liquid ingredients in a mixing glass with ice cubes and stir well. Strain into a chilled cocktail glass and garnish with lemon twist.

BLUE-ON-BLUE MARTINI

6 parts vodka

1 part blue curaçao

1 dash Angostura bitters

Cocktail olive

Combine liquid ingredients in a cocktail shaker with cracked ice and shake well. Strain into a chilled cocktail glass and garnish with olive.

Dry Humor

A man runs into a bar, orders four martinis at a time, and has the bartender line them up in front of him. He quickly throws them back, one after the other.

"Geez," the bartender says, "looks like you're in a rush."

"You would be too if you had what I have."

"What do you have?" the bartender asks, concerned.

"Fifty cents."

BOARDWALK

6 parts vodka

2 parts dry vermouth

½ teaspoon maraschino liqueur

1 teaspoon fresh lemon juice

Lemon twist

Combine liquid ingredients in a cocktail shaker with cracked ice and shake well. Strain into a chilled cocktail glass and garnish with lemon twist.

A Dry One

The search—some might say obsession—for the driest martini continues. For those who want just a whisper of vermouth, there are vermouth atomizers and even olives marinated in vermouth.

The driest martini is straight gin alone, but even those have been sent back to the bartender for not being dry enough.

BOOMERANG MARTINI ➤

6 parts gin

1 dash Angostura bitters

2 parts dry vermouth

1 dash maraschino liqueur

Kiwi slice

Stir all liquid ingredients with ice cubes in a mixing glass. Strain into a chilled cocktail glass and garnish with kiwi slice.

BROADWAY MARTINI

6 parts gin

1 part white crème de menthe

Fresh mint sprig

Combine liquid ingredients in a cocktail shaker with cracked ice and shake well. Strain into a chilled cocktail glass and garnish with mint sprig.

 Did You Know?

In the 1940s, John Lardner reported that the New York Yankees ball club had hired private detectives to keep track of their players. He noted that they "should have been easy to stalk because, belonging to a high-class ball club, they drank martinis and left a trail of olives."

BRONX TERRACE COCKTAIL

6 parts gin

2 parts fresh lime juice

1 part dry vermouth

Maraschino cherry

Combine liquid ingredients in a cocktail shaker with cracked ice and shake well. Strain into a chilled cocktail glass and garnish with cherry.

BROWN COCKTAIL ⇥

4 parts gin

2 parts light rum

1 part dry vermouth

Kumquat

Stir all ingredients in a mixing glass with cracked ice. Strain into a chilled cocktail glass and garnish with kumquat.

BUCKEYE MARTINI

6 parts gin

1 part dry vermouth

Black olive

Combine liquid ingredients in a cocktail shaker with cracked ice and shake well. Strain into a chilled cocktail glass and garnish with black olive.

CABARET MARTINI

6 parts gin

3 parts Dubonnet rouge

3 to 5 dashes Angostura bitters

3 to 5 dashes Pernod

Lime twist

Combine liquid ingredients in a cocktail shaker with cracked ice and shake well. Strain into a chilled cocktail glass and garnish with lime twist.

CAJUN MARTINI ⚓

6 parts pepper vodka

1 dash of dry vermouth

Olive stuffed with pickled jalapeño pepper

Combine liquid ingredients in a mixing glass with cracked ice and stir. Strain into a chilled cocktail glass and garnish with jalapeño-stuffed olive.

CALIFORNIA MARTINI

6 parts vodka

1 part red wine

1 tablespoon orange rum

3 to 5 dashes orange bitters

Orange twist

Combine liquid ingredients in a cocktail shaker with cracked ice and shake well. Strain into a chilled cocktail glass and garnish with orange twist.

CAMPARI MARTINI ⚓

6 parts vodka

1 part Campari

Lime twist

Combine liquid ingredients in a cocktail shaker with cracked ice and shake well. Strain into a chilled cocktail glass and garnish with lime twist.

CARIBOU MARTINI ⚓

4 parts coffee-flavored vodka, chilled

Champagne or dry sparkling wine

Lemon twist

Coffee bean

Pour chilled vodka into a cocktail glass. Top off with champagne and stir gently. Garnish with lemon twist and drop in the coffee bean.

CHOCOLATE CHERRY VELVETINI

½ ounce chocolate syrup

2 ounces chocolate-flavored liqueur

2 ounces cherry wine

2 ounces vodka

Chocolate-covered cherries

Drizzle the chocolate syrup into a chilled cocktail glass. Combine the liquid ingredients in a cocktail shaker with cracked ice and shake vigorously. Strain into the cocktail glass and garnish with chocolate-covered cherries.

CHOCOLATE CRUSH MARTINI

Cocoa powder, for the rim of the glass

1½ ounces chocolate-orange flavored vodka (or 1 ounce chocolate-flavored vodka and ½ ounce orange-flavored vodka)

Orange twist and dark chocolate truffle on a decorative skewer

Moisten the outer rim of a chilled cocktail glass and dip it in cocoa powder. Place vodka (or combination of vodkas) in a cocktail shaker with cracked ice and shake well. Strain into glass and garnish with orange twist and chocolate truffle.

> **"I feel sorry for people who don't drink. When they wake up in the morning, that's the best they are going to feel all day."**
>
> —DEAN MARTIN

CHOCOLATE MARTINI ➻

6 parts vodka

1 part chocolate liqueur

Chocolate curl

Combine vodka and liqueur in a mixing glass with ice cubes and stir. Strain into a chilled cocktail glass and garnish with chocolate curl.

CHRISTMAS MARTINI

6 parts gin

1 part dry vermouth

1 teaspoon peppermint schnapps

Miniature candy cane

Combine liquid ingredients in a cocktail shaker with cracked ice and shake well. Strain into a chilled cocktail glass and garnish with candy cane.

CHRISTMAS 'TINI

6 parts vodka

1 part dry vermouth

1 teaspoon peppermint schnapps

Miniature candy cane

Combine liquid ingredients in a cocktail shaker with cracked ice and shake well. Strain into a chilled cocktail glass and garnish with candy cane.

Did You Know?

Winston Churchill was a martini aficionado. His signature martini was not unlike that of most fans of the extremely dry martini. Some people whisper "vermouth." Others, like Churchill, simply look at the bottle.

CHURCHILL'S MARTINI

6 parts gin
Bottle of dry vermouth
Cocktail olive

Shake gin in a cocktail shaker with cracked ice. Strain into a chilled cocktail glass and look at the bottle of vermouth. Garnish glass with olive.

CHURCH LADY MARTINI ➥

4 parts gin
2 parts dry vermouth
2 parts fresh orange juice
Lemon, lime, and orange wedges

Combine liquid ingredients in a cocktail shaker with cracked ice and shake well. Strain into a chilled cocktail glass. Garnish with fruit wedges.

> **"Do not allow children to mix drinks. It is unseemly and they use too much vermouth."**
>
> —STEVE ALLEN

CITRUS MARTINI ❦

8 parts lemon-flavored vodka
1 teaspoon Grand Marnier or orange liqueur
1 teaspoon fresh lime juice
Lemon twist

Combine liquid ingredients in a cocktail shaker with cracked ice and shake well. Strain into a chilled cocktail glass and garnish with lemon twist.

CLEMENTINI

3 ounces orange-flavored vodka

½ ounce Grand Marnier or orange liqueur

1 ounce fresh clementine juice (see note)

Clementine segments

Combine liquid ingredients in a cocktail shaker with cracked ice and shake well. Strain into a chilled cocktail glass and garnish with clementine segments.

NOTE: FOR A VARIATION THAT'S A BIT MORE FUN TO MIX UP, YOU CAN SUBSTITUTE THE CLEMENTINE JUICE WITH A PEELED FRESH CLEMENTINE. MUDDLE THE CLEMENTINE IN THE SHAKER, ADD THE ICE AND THE OTHER LIQUIDS, AND PROCEED AS DIRECTED.

COFFEE LOVER'S MARTINI ♟

6 parts coffee-flavored vodka

1 part dry vermouth

1 part Frangelico

Coffee beans

Combine liquid ingredients in a cocktail shaker with cracked ice and shake well. Strain into a chilled cocktail glass and garnish with a few coffee beans.

COLD COMFORT MARTINI ❧

4 parts lemon vodka
4 parts honey vodka
Lemon twist

Here's a martini to conquer the flu: Combine vodkas in a cocktail
shaker with cracked ice and shake well. Strain into a chilled cocktail
glass and garnish with lemon twist.

COLONY CLUB MARTINI

6 parts gin

1 teaspoon Pernod

3 to 5 dashes orange bitters

Orange twist

Combine liquid ingredients in a cocktail shaker with cracked ice and shake well. Strain into a chilled cocktail glass and garnish with orange twist.

"As you empty the bottles you refill them with your soul."

—GERARD DE NERVAL

COSMOPOLITAN

4 parts vodka

2 parts triple sec

2 parts cranberry juice

1 part fresh lime juice

Combine ingredients in a cocktail shaker with cracked ice and shake well. Strain into a chilled cocktail glass.

CRANTINI ➼

6 parts gin

1 part unsweetened cranberry juice

Lime or lemon twist

Pour gin into a chilled cocktail glass. Slowly add the cranberry juice. Garnish with lime or lemon twist.

CRIME OF PASSION MARTINI

2 ounces Alize

½ ounce vodka

½ ounce cranberry juice

Orange twist

Combine liquid ingredients in a cocktail shaker with cracked ice and shake well. Strain into a chilled cocktail glass and garnish with the orange twist.

"Yes, I'd like a cheeseburger, please, large fries and a Cosmopolitan."
—CARRIE BRADSHAW, *SEX AND THE CITY*

It is said that Hemingway used to drink a Montgomery—a martini with a gin-to-vermouth ratio of 15 to 1. Supposedly the drink was named after World War II hero Field Marshall Montgomery—the ratio being the same as the odds he sought before entering battle.

CRIMSON MARTINI ⤙

6 parts gin

1 part ruby port

2 teaspoons fresh lime juice

1 teaspoon grenadine

Lime twist

Combine liquid ingredients in a cocktail shaker with cracked ice and shake well. Strain into a chilled cocktail glass and garnish with lime twist.

CUBAN MARTINI

Granulated sugar, for the rim of the glass

6 parts light rum

1 part dry vermouth

Lime twist

Rim a chilled cocktail glass with sugar. Combine liquid ingredients in a cocktail shaker with cracked ice and shake well. Strain into cocktail glass and garnish with lime twist.

DANISH MARTINI

6 parts aquavit

1 part dry vermouth

Cocktail olive

Combine liquid ingredients in a cocktail shaker with cracked ice and shake well. Strain into a chilled cocktail glass and garnish with olive.

DARLIN' CLEMENTINE

2 ounces sour apple schnapps

1 ounce gin

1 ounce coconut rum

1 ounce vodka

1 splash orange juice

Clementine wedge

Combine liquid ingredients in a cocktail shaker with ice cubes. Shake well and strain into a chilled cocktail glass. Garnish with clementine wedge.

DAYDREAM MARTINI

6 parts citrus vodka

1 part triple sec

2 parts fresh orange juice

¼ teaspoon bar sugar

Combine all ingredients in a mixing glass with cracked ice and stir well. Strain into a chilled cocktail glass.

Dry Humor

Charles Dickens walks into a bar and orders a martini.

The bartender asks, "Olive or twist?"

It is said that Jackie Gleason once ordered a martini at a bar in a fashionable Miami Beach hotel. When the bartender asked him if he wanted a twist of lemon with it, he exclaimed, "When I want a goddam lemonade, I'll ask for it!"

DEEP SEA MARTINI

6 parts gin

2 parts dry vermouth

½ teaspoon Pernod

1 dash orange bitters

Combine all ingredients in a mixing glass with cracked ice and stir well. Strain into a chilled cocktail glass.

DELICIOUS MARTINI

6 parts coffee-flavored vodka

1 part Grand Marnier

Orange twist

Combine liquid ingredients in a cocktail shaker with cracked ice and shake well. Strain into a chilled cocktail glass and garnish with orange twist.

DESPERATE MARTINI

6 parts gin

1 part dry vermouth

1 part blackberry brandy

Fresh blackberries (optional)

Combine liquid ingredients in a cocktail shaker with cracked ice and shake well. Strain into a chilled cocktail glass and garnish with fresh blackberries.

DIRTY MARTINI

6 parts gin

2 parts dry vermouth

1 part olive brine

Cocktail olives

Combine liquid ingredients in a cocktail shaker with cracked ice and shake well. Strain into a chilled cocktail glass and garnish with one or two olives.

DIRTY VODKA MARTINI

6 parts vodka

2 parts dry vermouth

1 part olive brine

Cocktail olives

Combine liquid ingredients in a cocktail shaker with cracked ice and shake well. Strain into a chilled cocktail glass and garnish with one or two olives.

> "Happiness is finding two olives in your martini when you're hungry."
> —JOHNNY CARSON

DOUBLE FUDGE MARTINI

6 parts vodka

1 part chocolate liqueur

1 part coffee liqueur

Chocolate cocktail straw

Combine liquid ingredients in a mixing glass with cracked ice and stir well. Strain into a chilled cocktail glass and garnish with chocolate straw.

EAST WING

6 parts vodka

1 part Campari

2 parts cherry brandy

Lemon twist

Combine liquid ingredients in a cocktail shaker with cracked ice and shake well. Strain into a chilled cocktail glass and garnish with lemon twist.

EAT MY MARTINI

6 parts honey vodka

1 part amontillado sherry

Almond-stuffed olive

Combine liquid ingredients in a cocktail shaker with cracked ice and shake well. Strain into a chilled cocktail glass and garnish with almond-stuffed olive.

EMERALD MARTINI ➻

6 parts citrus-flavored vodka

2 parts chartreuse

Lemon twist

Lime twist

Combine liquid ingredients in a mixing glass with cracked ice and stir well. Strain into a chilled cocktail glass and garnish with lemon and lime twists.

EXTRA DRY VODKA MARTINI

4 parts vodka

3 to 5 drops dry vermouth

⅛ teaspoon lemon juice

Lemon twist

Combine liquid ingredients in a cocktail shaker with cracked ice and shake well. Strain into a chilled cocktail glass and garnish with lemon twist.

A Few Too Many?

W.H. Auden often prepared for his lectures with a few martinis. On one occasion in 1947, he had a few too many before he spoke at Harvard. The topic was supposed to have been Miguel de Cervantes, but when Auden stood up at the podium, he apologized for his new dentures and then told the eager crowd that he'd never been able to read *Don Quixote* to the end, and bet that no one in the audience had either.

Nick and Nora Charles, the sophisticated sleuthing couple from *The Thin Man* novels and movies, were dyed-in-the-wool martini drinkers. Nick used to measure out the vermouth with an eyedropper.

FARE THEE WELL MARTINI

6 parts gin

1 part dry vermouth

1 dash sweet vermouth

1 dash Cointreau

Combine all ingredients in a mixing glass with cracked ice and stir well. Strain into a chilled cocktail glass.

FARMER'S MARTINI

6 parts gin

1 part dry vermouth

1 part sweet vermouth

3 to 5 dashes Angostura bitters

Combine all ingredients in a cocktail shaker with cracked ice and shake well. Strain into a chilled cocktail glass.

Did You Know?

Franklin D. Roosevelt was a serious martini drinker and carried a martini kit with him whenever he traveled. During the Tehran Conference, he insisted on mixing one of his specialties for Joseph Stalin. Stalin found it "cold on the stomach" but liked it. FDR's martini was most likely the first "Dirty Martini."

FDR'S MARTINI

2 parts gin

1 part vermouth

1 teaspoon olive brine

Lemon twist

Cocktail olive

Rub the lemon twist around the rim of a chilled cocktail glass and discard the peel. Combine gin, vermouth, and olive brine in a cocktail shaker with cracked ice and shake well. Strain into chilled glass and garnish with olive.

FESTIVAL ESPRESSO MARTINI

1 part brewed espresso, chilled

1 part Kahlua

1 part coffee-flavored vodka

1 part vanilla-flavored vodka

Combine all ingredients in a cocktail shaker with ice and shake well. Strain into a chilled cocktail glass.

FIFTY-FIFTY MARTINI

4 parts gin

4 parts dry vermouth

Cocktail olive

Combine liquid ingredients in a mixing glass with cracked ice and stir well. Strain into a chilled cocktail glass and garnish with olive.

FIFTY-FIFTY VODKA MARTINI

4 parts vodka

4 parts dry vermouth

Cocktail olive

Combine liquid ingredients in a mixing glass with cracked ice and stir well. Strain into a chilled cocktail glass and garnish with olive.

FINE AND DANDY

4 parts gin

2 parts triple sec

2 parts fresh lemon juice

1 dash orange bitters

Combine all ingredients in a cocktail shaker with cracked ice and shake well. Strain into a chilled cocktail glass.

FINO MARTINI

6 parts gin or vodka

1 teaspoon fino sherry

Lemon twist

Combine liquid ingredients in a mixing glass with ice cubes and stir well. Strain into a chilled cocktail glass and garnish with lemon twist.

 Did You Know?

The martini reached the height of popularity in the 1950s. One Manhattan bar served martinis "dry, extra dry, or very dry." The drier the martini, the more the drink cost.

"Martinis should always be stirred, not shaken, so that the molecules lie sensuously one on top of the other."

—W. SOMERSET MAUGHAM

FLIRTINI

5 fresh raspberries

1 ounce raspberry-flavored vodka

½ ounce orange liqueur

½ ounce pineapple juice

Splash of fresh lime juice

Champagne or sparkling wine

Muddle the raspberries in a chilled cocktail glass. Combine liquid ingredients in a cocktail shaker with cracked ice, shake well, and strain into the cocktail glass. Slowly top off with champagne or sparkling wine.

FRETFUL MARTINI

6 parts gin

1 part blue curaçao

1 dash Angostura bitters

Cocktail olive

Combine liquid ingredients in a cocktail shaker with cracked ice and shake well. Strain into a chilled cocktail glass and garnish with olive.

FROSTY MANGO MARTINI

2 ounces mango nectar

2 ounces vodka

1 ounce triple sec

¼ ounce Rose's lime juice

1 cup cracked ice

Mango slice

Place liquid ingredients and ice in a blender and blend at high speed until combined and frothy. Pour into a chilled cocktail glass and garnish with a mango slice.

FROZEN MARTINI

5 parts gin

1 part dry vermouth

2 almond-stuffed cocktail olives

Place gin, vermouth, olives, cocktail glass, and cocktail shaker in freezer for at least three hours. When all components are thoroughly chilled, combine gin and vermouth in the chilled cocktail shaker and shake well. Place the two frozen olives in the chilled cocktail glass and pour the gin and vermouth mixture over it.

FUZZY MARTINI

4 parts vanilla-flavored vodka

1 part coffee-flavored vodka

1 teaspoon peach schnapps

Fresh peach slice

Combine liquid ingredients in a mixing glass with ice cubes and stir well. Strain into a chilled cocktail glass and garnish with a fresh peach slice.

GIBSON ♟

8 parts gin or vodka

3 to 5 dashes dry vermouth

2 cocktail onions

Combine liquid ingredients in a mixing glass with ice cubes and stir well. Strain into a chilled cocktail glass and garnish with onions.

The Gibson is thought to have been named for the famed Gibson Girls, Charles Dana Gibson's lovely pinups of the early twentieth century. The two cocktail onions are believed to represent breasts.

GILROY MARTINI

6 parts buffalo grass vodka

2 parts dry vermouth

2 drops garlic juice

Garlic-stuffed olive

Combine liquid ingredients in a cocktail shaker with cracked ice and shake well. Strain into a chilled cocktail glass and garnish with garlic-stuffed olive.

GIMLET ↣

8 parts gin or vodka

2 parts Rose's lime juice

Combine all ingredients in a cocktail shaker with cracked ice and shake well. Strain into a chilled cocktail glass.

A Timeless Drink

The martini is a thoroughly modern cocktail. Even though the drink was most likely invented in the nineteenth century, it did not gain popularity until well into the twentieth century, and it really took off after Prohibition. Sweeter drinks lost their appeal after World War II, and the already dry martini got even drier. By the mid-1950s, the true mark of a sophisticate was a dry, icy gin martini, with only a trace of vermouth.

GIN AND IT

8 parts gin

2 parts sweet vermouth

Lemon twist

Combine liquid ingredients in a cocktail shaker with cracked ice and shake well. Strain into a chilled cocktail glass and garnish with lemon twist.

GINGER SNAP MARTINI

1½ ounces vodka

½ teaspoon ginger syrup

1-inch piece freshly cut ginger

½ ounce ginger ale

Thin slice fresh ginger

Combine the vodka and ginger syrup in a cocktail shaker half full of cracked ice and let stand to chill. Rub the inside and rim of a chilled cocktail glass with the cut side of the fresh ginger piece. Shake the vodka and ginger syrup well and strain into the cocktail glass. Slowly add the ginger ale. Garnish with ginger slice.

GOLDEN DELICIOUS ➥ MARTINI

2 parts vodka

1 part apple schnapps

Splash of fresh lime juice

Apple slice

Combine liquid ingredients in a cocktail shaker with cracked ice and shake or stir. Strain into a chilled cocktail glass and garnish with apple slice.

"When I have one martini, I feel bigger, wiser, taller. When I have a second, I feel superlative. When I have more, there's no holding me."

—WILLIAM FAULKNER

The last shot of the day on a movie set is called the "martini shot."

GOLF MARTINI

8 parts gin

3 to 5 dashes Angostura bitters

2 parts dry vermouth

Cocktail olive

Combine liquid ingredients in a mixing glass with cracked ice and shake well. Strain into a chilled cocktail glass and garnish with olive.

GREAT CAESAR'S MARTINI

6 parts vodka

1 part dry vermouth

Anchovy-stuffed olive

Combine liquid ingredients in a cocktail shaker with cracked ice and shake well. Strain into a chilled cocktail glass and garnish with anchovy-stuffed olive.

Dry Humor

A man arrives at a restaurant several minutes before his wife to instruct the head waiter, "No matter what kind of soup I order, fill the tureen with martinis. My wife has a fit if I order even one drink." His instructions were carried out; the man then called to the waiter, "I'll have some more soup, and this time, make it extra dry."

Did You Know?

The original recipe for the dry martini actually wasn't very dry by today's standards. The proportions were two parts gin to one part French or dry vermouth.

GREEN MARTINI

6 parts gin

1 part chartreuse

Almond-stuffed olive

Combine liquid ingredients in a cocktail shaker with cracked ice and shake well. Strain into a chilled cocktail glass and garnish with almond-stuffed olive.

GREEN TEANI

1 ounce green tea, chilled

2 ounces citrus-flavored vodka

1 teaspoon triple sec

1 teaspoon simple syrup (see page 22)

Orange twist

Combine liquid ingredients in a cocktail shaker with cracked ice. Shake well and strain into a chilled cocktail glass. Garnish with orange twist.

GUMDROP MARTINI

4 parts lemon-flavored rum

2 parts vodka

1 part Southern Comfort

½ teaspoon dry vermouth

1 part fresh lemon juice

Bar sugar

Lemon slice

Gumdrops

Rim a chilled cocktail glass with bar sugar. Combine liquid ingredients in a cocktail shaker with cracked ice and shake well. Strain into the chilled cocktail glass and garnish with lemon slice and gumdrops.

GYPSY MARTINI �

8 parts gin

2 parts sweet vermouth

Maraschino cherry

Combine liquid ingredients in a cocktail shaker with cracked ice and shake well. Strain into a chilled cocktail glass and garnish with cherry.

HASTY MARTINI

6 parts gin

1 part dry vermouth

3 to 5 dashes Pernod

1 teaspoon grenadine

Combine all ingredients in a cocktail shaker with cracked ice and shake well. Strain into a chilled cocktail glass.

HEP CAT

6 parts berry vodka

1 part dry vermouth

1 dash sweet vermouth

1 dash Cointreau

Combine all ingredients in a mixing glass with cracked ice and stir well. Strain into a chilled cocktail glass.

HOFFMAN HOUSE MARTINI

8 parts gin

1 part dry vermouth

3 to 5 dashes orange bitters

Cocktail olive

Combine liquid ingredients in a mixing glass with cracked ice and stir well. Strain into a chilled cocktail glass and garnish with olive.

> "For gin, in cruel sober truth, supplies the fuel for flaming youth."
>
> —NOEL COWARD

HOLLYWOOD MARTINI

6 parts gin

1 part Goldwasser

1 part dry vermouth

1 blue cheese-stuffed olive

Combine liquid ingredients in a cocktail shaker with cracked ice and shake well. Strain into a chilled cocktail glass and garnish with blue cheese-stuffed olive.

HOMESTEAD MARTINI ←«

6 parts gin

2 parts sweet vermouth

Orange twist

Combine liquid ingredients in a mixing glass with ice and stir well. Strain into a chilled cocktail glass and garnish with orange twist.

HONEYDEW MARTINI

6 parts vodka

1 part Midori

1 part triple sec

Lemon twist

Combine liquid ingredients in a cocktail shaker with cracked ice and shake well. Strain into a chilled cocktail glass and garnish with lemon twist.

Dry Humor

A guy walked into a bar and ordered a martini. Before tossing it back, he took out the olive and dropped it into a jar. He ordered another martini and again did the same thing—dropped the olive into the jar before drinking the martini. After an hour, the man was full of martinis and the jar was full of olives. He stumbled out of the bar and into the night.

Another customer turned to the bartender and said, "Strange—I never saw that before!"

"What's so strange?" said the bartender. "His wife sent him out for a jar of olives."

HOOSIER COCKTAIL

4 parts buffalo grass vodka

2 parts light rum

1 part dry vermouth

Combine all ingredients in a mixing glass with cracked ice and stir well. Strain into a chilled cocktail glass.

HOT AND DIRTY MARTINI ➺

6 parts pepper vodka

1 part dry vermouth

1 teaspoon olive brine

Olive stuffed with pickled jalapeño pepper

Combine liquid ingredients in a cocktail shaker with cracked ice and shake well. Strain into a chilled cocktail glass and garnish with jalapeño-stuffed olive.

HOT MAMA MARTINI

1½ ounces pepper-flavored vodka

3 drops cinnamon schnapps

Splash Rose's lime juice

Jalapeño pepper slice

Combine the liquid ingredients in a cocktail shaker with cracked ice and shake well. Strain into a chilled cocktail glass and garnish with jalapeño slice.

HOTEL PLAZA COCKTAIL

2 parts gin

2 parts dry vermouth

2 parts sweet vermouth

Maraschino cherry

Combine liquid ingredients in a mixing glass with ice cubes and stir well. Strain into a chilled cocktail glass and garnish with cherry.

ICY FRAPPUTINI

1 part brewed espresso, chilled

1 part Bailey's Irish Cream

1 part coffee-flavored vodka

Combine liquids in a cocktail shaker with cracked ice and shake very well. Strain into a chilled cocktail glass.

IDEAL MARTINI

6 parts gin

2 parts dry vermouth

$\frac{1}{2}$ teaspoon maraschino liqueur

1 teaspoon fresh lemon juice

Lemon twist

Combine liquid ingredients in a cocktail shaker with cracked ice and shake well. Strain into a chilled cocktail glass and garnish with lemon twist.

"A man must defend his home, his wife, his children and his martini."
—JACKIE GLEASON

IMPERIAL MARTINI 🍸

6 parts gin

2 parts dry vermouth

½ teaspoon maraschino liqueur

3 to 5 dashes Angostura bitters

Combine all ingredients in a mixing glass with ice and stir well. Strain into a chilled cocktail glass.

IN AND OUT MARTINI

7 parts vodka

Dry vermouth

2 blue cheese-stuffed olives

Lemon twist

"In and out" refers to the method of mixing this martini. Pour vermouth into a well-chilled martini glass. Swish it around and then discard. Pour vodka into the glass and garnish with blue cheese-stuffed olives and lemon twist.

A Fighting "Spirit"

In Havana, Ernest Hemingway had a many-martini lunch with the famous prizefighter Gene Tunney. As the two men got drunker, Hemingway got belligerent and tried to goad Tunney into a fight. (Hemingway considered himself quite the authority on boxing.) He kept punching at Tunney. Tunney, ever the gentleman, asked Hemingway to stop. But he would not. Finally, Tunney decided to give him a little "liver punch," just to get him to stop, and he let him have it. Hemingway buckled, his face went gray, and Tunney thought he was going to go out. But he didn't, and after that, Hemingway was the perfect gentleman for the rest of the afternoon.

IRISH MARTINI

Irish whiskey

6 parts buffalo grass vodka

1 part dry vermouth

Lemon twist

Rinse a chilled cocktail glass with Irish whiskey; discard (or drink!) the excess. Combine vodka and vermouth in a cocktail shaker with cracked ice and shake well. Strain into cocktail glass and garnish with lemon twist.

ISLAND MARTINI

6 parts gold rum

1 part dry vermouth

1 part sweet vermouth

Lemon twist

Combine liquid ingredients in a cocktail shaker with cracked ice and shake well. Strain into a chilled cocktail glass and garnish with lemon twist.

JACK LONDON MARTINI

6 parts currant vodka

2 parts Dubonnet blanc

1 part maraschino liqueur

Lemon twist

Combine liquid ingredients in a cocktail shaker with cracked ice and shake well. Strain into a chilled cocktail glass and garnish with lemon twist.

JAMAICAN MARTINI ⚓

6 parts gin

1 part red wine

1 tablespoon dark rum

3 to 5 dashes orange bitters

Cherry peppers

Combine liquid ingredients in a cocktail shaker with cracked ice and shake well. Strain into a chilled cocktail glass and garnish with cherry peppers.

JAMES BOND MARTINI ✈

6 parts gin
2 parts vodka
1 part Lillet blanc
Lemon twist

Combine liquid ingredients in a cocktail shaker with cracked ice and shake well. Strain into a chilled cocktail glass and garnish with lemon twist.

JAMIE'S MARTINI

6 parts vodka
1 part triple sec
2 parts fresh orange juice
¼ teaspoon bar sugar

Combine all ingredients in a mixing glass with cracked ice and stir well. Strain into a chilled cocktail glass.

JOURNALIST MARTINI

6 parts gin
1 teaspoon dry vermouth
1 teaspoon sweet vermouth
1 teaspoon triple sec
1 teaspoon fresh lime juice
1 dash Angostura bitters

Combine all ingredients in a cocktail shaker with cracked ice and shake well. Strain into a chilled cocktail glass.

JUICY TANGERINI

¼ tangerine

2 ounces orange-flavored vodka

1 ounce fresh lemon juice

1 ounce simple syrup (see page 22)

Granulated sugar, for the rim of the glass

Tangerine twist

Fill a cocktail glass with ice and let chill. Squeeze juice from tangerine into a cocktail shaker with cracked ice and drop tangerine into shaker. Add liquid ingredients and shake well. Empty the now-chilled cocktail glass and dip the outer rim in sugar. Strain the martini into the chilled glass and garnish with tangerine twist.

KEY LIME PIE MARTINI

1 key lime or lime wedge

Graham cracker crumbs, for the rim of the glass

3 ounces vanilla-flavored vodka

¼ cup key lime liqueur

1 ounce pineapple juice

1 ounce heavy whipping cream

Key lime or lime slice

Moisten the rim of a cocktail glass with the lime and dip the outer rim in the graham cracker crumbs. Chill the glass for at least 30 minutes. Combine liquid ingredients in a cocktail shaker with cracked ice and shake well. Strain into prepared martini glass and garnish with key lime slice.

An Interesting Theory

H.L. Mencken usually drank beer but made an exception when he spent an evening with prominent New Yorker Philip Goodman. When Mencken came up to New York from Baltimore, he and Goodman would go to a speakeasy in Union City, New Jersey, and eat a dinner of knockwurst, boiled beef, sauerkraut, mashed potatoes, and cheesecake. They would wash this down with several beers and coffees. They would then return to Manhattan, stop at a restaurant on West Forty-Fourth Street, have more cheesecake and some strudel, and more coffee and more beer. They would always end the evening by having double martinis. Goodman believed that the gin aided digestion—that it "oxidized" the food.

> "Give strong drink unto him that is ready to perish and wine unto those that be of heavy hearts. Let him drink and forget his poverty and remember his misery no more."
>
> —PROVERBS 31:6-7

KIWI KISS MARTINI

2 ounce vodka

½ ounce kiwi liqueur

Splash of fresh lemon juice

Kiwi slice

Combine liquid ingredients in a cocktail shaker with cracked ice and shake well. Strain into a chilled cocktail glass and garnish with kiwi slice.

KNICKERBOCKER

6 parts gin

2 parts dry vermouth

½ teaspoon sweet vermouth

Lemon twist

Combine liquid ingredients in a mixing glass with cracked ice and stir well. Strain into a chilled cocktail glass and garnish with lemon twist.

KUP'S INDISPENSABLE MARTINI

6 parts gin

1½ parts dry vermouth

1½ parts sweet vermouth

Orange twist

Combine liquid ingredients in a cocktail shaker with cracked ice and shake well. Strain into a chilled cocktail glass and garnish with orange twist.

> "After four martinis, my husband turns into a disgusting beast. And after the fifth, I pass out altogether."
>
> —ANONYMOUS

KYOTO ➤

6 parts gin

2 parts melon liqueur

Melon ball

1 part dry vermouth

¼ teaspoon fresh lemon juice

Combine liquid ingredients in a mixing glass with ice cubes and stir well. Strain into a chilled cocktail glass and garnish with melon ball.

LEAP YEAR MARTINI

6 parts citrus-flavored vodka

1 part sweet vermouth

1 part Grand Marnier

½ teaspoon fresh lemon juice

Combine all ingredients in a cocktail shaker with cracked ice and shake well. Strain into a chilled cocktail glass.

Y | Did You Know?

Sylvia Plath, Anne Sexton, and George Starbuck all took Robert Lowell's creative writing course at the Boston Center for Adult Education. After each class, they would pile into Sexton's old Ford, drive to the Ritz Hotel, and park illegally in a loading zone—Sexton explaining, "It's OK, we're only going to get loaded." They then proceeded into the Ritz to have three or four martinis each.

LEMON DROP MARTINI ⊷

6 parts lemon-flavored vodka

1 part dry vermouth

Granulated sugar

Lemon twist

Moisten the outer rim of a cocktail glass and dip it in granulated sugar. Combine liquid ingredients in a cocktail shaker with cracked ice and shake well. Strain into cocktail glass and garnish with lemon twist.

LEMON PUCKER

Lemon wedge

2 teaspoons sugar, divided

2 ounces lemon or unflavored vodka

2 teaspoons fresh lemon juice

Lemon slice

Run the lemon wedge around the outer rim of a chilled cocktail glass to moisten it, then dip the rim in one teaspoon of the sugar. Combine the remaining teaspoon sugar and liquid ingredients in a cocktail shaker with cracked ice and shake well. Strain into a chilled cocktail glass and garnish with lemon slice.

LEMON TWIST ❦

6 parts lemon-flavored rum
1 part dry vermouth
Lemon twist

Combine liquid ingredients in a cocktail shaker with cracked ice and shake well. Strain into a chilled cocktail glass and garnish with lemon twist.

LONDON MARTINI ➻

6 parts gin
½ teaspoon maraschino liqueur
3 to 5 dashes orange bitters
½ teaspoon bar sugar
Cucumber twist
Cocktail olives

Combine liquid ingredients in a mixing glass and stir well. Pour mixture into a cocktail shaker with cracked ice and shake well. Strain into a chilled cocktail glass and garnish with cucumber twist and olives.

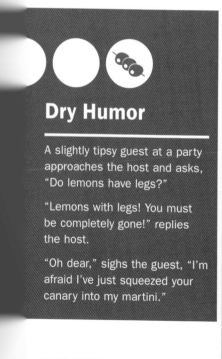

Dry Humor

A slightly tipsy guest at a party approaches the host and asks, "Do lemons have legs?"

"Lemons with legs! You must be completely gone!" replies the host.

"Oh dear," sighs the guest, "I'm afraid I've just squeezed your canary into my martini."

LOW TIDE MARTINI

6 parts vodka

1 part dry vermouth

Lime twist

1 teaspoon clam juice

Olive stuffed with smoked clam

Combine liquid ingredients in a cocktail shaker with cracked ice and shake well. Strain into a chilled cocktail glass and garnish with clam-stuffed olive.

LYCHEE MARTINI

3 ounces vodka

¼ ounce lychee syrup

1 lychee, peeled and pitted

Combine liquid ingredients in a cocktail shaker with cracked ice. Shake well, strain into a chilled cocktail glass, and garnish with lychee.

MACAROON

6 parts vodka

1 part chocolate liqueur

1 part amaretto

Orange twist

Combine liquid ingredients in a mixing glass with cracked ice and stir well. Strain into a chilled cocktail glass and garnish with orange twist.

MAMA'S MARTINI

6 parts vanilla vodka

1 part apricot brandy

3 to 5 dashes Angostura bitters

3 to 5 dashes lemon juice

Combine all ingredients in a cocktail shaker with cracked ice and shake well. Strain into a chilled cocktail glass.

MANHASSET ♠

6 parts rye whiskey

½ part dry vermouth

½ part sweet vermouth

1 tablespoon fresh lemon juice

Lemon twist

Combine liquid ingredients in a cocktail shaker with cracked ice and shake well. Strain into a chilled cocktail glass and garnish with lemon twist.

Shaken Not Stirred

James Bond's vodka martini—"shaken not stirred"—was a radical concept when Ian Fleming introduced it as a "Vesper" in *Casino Royale*. A typical martini was never shaken, and it had to be made with gin. But who could argue with James Bond? His Vesper started a martini revolution. Today, much to purists' chagrin, vodka martinis are more popular than the original gin cocktail.

MANHATTAN ➤

6 parts rye whiskey

2 parts sweet vermouth

1 dash Angostura bitters

Maraschino cherry

Combine liquid ingredients in a mixing glass with ice and stir well. Strain into a chilled cocktail glass and garnish with cherry.

MARITIME MARTINI

6 parts gin

2 parts dry vermouth

Anchovy-stuffed olive

Combine liquid ingredients in a cocktail shaker with cracked ice and shake well. Strain into a chilled cocktail glass and garnish with anchovy-stuffed olive.

Did You Know?

A Manhattan is thought to be the "opposite" of a martini. While a martini is made with clear liquor, gin or vodka, and dry vermouth, a Manhattan is made with amber whiskey and sweet vermouth (and don't forget the bitters)! Is a cherry really the opposite of an olive?

A California Native

Some say the martini was developed in Europe, others say it was New York. But others still believe that this elegant drink had its not so elegant beginnings in the 1860s, in California, after the Gold Rush. According to legend, the martini was invented by a man about to hop on the ferry from Martinez, California, to San Francisco. He needed some fortification for the journey across the Bay. All there was at hand was some rotgut gin. To take the burn off the gin, he mixed it with an equal part of vermouth and sweetened it with a few drops of maraschino and orange bitters. And the martini, or "Martinez Cocktail," was born—a California native.

MARTINEZ COCKTAIL

4 parts gin

2 parts sweet vermouth

1 part maraschino liqueur

1 teaspoon simple syrup (optional, see page 22)

1 to 3 dashes Angostura bitters

Combine all ingredients in a mixing glass with cracked ice and stir well. Strain into a chilled old-fashioned glass.

MARTINI MILANO

4 parts gin

1 part dry vermouth

1 part dry white wine

1 teaspoon Campari

Lime twist

Combine liquid ingredients in a cocktail shaker with cracked ice and shake well. Strain into a chilled cocktail glass and garnish with lime twist.

MARTINI NAVRATILOVA

6 parts vodka

2 parts dry vermouth

3 to 5 dashes orange bitters

Combine all ingredients in a cocktail shaker with cracked ice and shake well. Strain into a chilled cocktail glass.

MARTUNIA ⚓

6 parts gin

1 part dry vermouth

1 part sweet vermouth

Edible flowers (organic)

Combine liquid ingredients in a cocktail shaker with cracked ice and shake well. Strain into a chilled cocktail glass and garnish with edible flowers.

♈ | Did You Know?

The Ritz bar in Paris was and is a favorite haunt of many literary figures. James Jones and William Styron once spent all night getting drunk and continued into the next day. They ended up at the Ritz at noon, drinking straight-up martinis. At about three in the afternoon, they decided to call it a night.

METROPOLITAN ⊷

6 parts currant vodka

1 part Lillet blanc

½ teaspoon fresh lime juice

Lemon twist

Combine liquid ingredients in a cocktail shaker with cracked ice and shake well. Strain into a chilled cocktail glass and garnish with lemon twist.

MOCHA BLANCA MARTINI

6 parts coffee-flavored vodka

2 parts white chocolate liqueur

White chocolate curl

Combine liquid ingredients in a mixing glass and stir well. Strain into a chilled cocktail glass and garnish with white chocolate curl.

MOLL FLANDERS

4 parts gin

2 parts sloe gin

2 parts dry vermouth

3 to 5 dashes Angostura bitters

Combine all ingredients in a mixing glass with cracked ice and stir well. Strain into a chilled cocktail glass.

> "Connoisseurs who like their martinis very dry suggest simply allowing a ray of sunlight to shine through the bottle of Noilly Prat before it hits the gin."
>
> —LUIS BUÑUEL

NAKED MARTINI

6 parts gin

Cocktail olive

Chill gin in freezer for at least two hours. Pour gin into a chilled cocktail glass and garnish with olive.

NEGRONI

4 parts gin

2 parts Campari

1 part sweet vermouth

Orange twist

Combine liquid ingredients in a cocktail shaker with cracked ice and shake well. Strain into a chilled cocktail glass and garnish with orange twist.

An Interesting Observation

The writer John Lardner once posited that the drinks of primitive people are apt to be sweet and thick. The martini, then, represents the most advanced and sophisticated civilization, since it is clear, cold, thin, and dry. The ultimate martini is the Naked Martini—the zenith of a civilization.

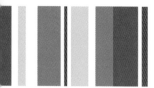

NEWBURY

6 parts gin

2 parts sweet vermouth

1 part triple sec

Lemon twist

Combine liquid ingredients in a cocktail shaker with cracked ice and shake well. Strain into a chilled cocktail glass and garnish with lemon twist.

NEW ORLEANS MARTINI

6 parts vanilla vodka

1 parts dry vermouth

1 part Pernod

1 dash Angostura bitters

Fresh mint sprig

Combine liquid ingredients in a cocktail shaker with cracked ice and shake well. Strain into a chilled cocktail glass and garnish with mint sprig.

NIGHTMARE

6 parts gin

2 parts Madeira wine

2 parts cherry brandy

Orange twist

Combine liquid ingredients in a mixing glass with cracked ice and stir well. Strain into a chilled cocktail glass and garnish with orange twist.

NINOTCHKA

6 parts vanilla-flavored vodka

2 parts white chocolate liqueur

1 part fresh lemon juice

Combine all ingredients in a cocktail shaker with cracked ice and shake well. Strain into a chilled cocktail glass.

NORTHERN LIGHTS MARTINI

6 parts currant-flavored vodka

1 teaspoon Chambord liqueur

Juniper berries soaked in vermouth

Combine liquid ingredients in a cocktail shaker with cracked ice and shake well. Strain into a chilled cocktail glass and garnish with juniper berries.

NUTTY MARTINI

6 parts vodka

1 part Frangelico

Lemon twist

Combine liquid ingredients in a cocktail shaker with cracked ice and shake well. Strain into a chilled cocktail glass and garnish with lemon twist.

The Roundtable

The writers of the famed Algonquin Roundtable loved their martin But when they gathered in the Rose Room, Prohibition was law, the Algonquin Hotel was legally dry. To alleviate this problem, aft a meal, the denizens of the Roundtable would visit their friend, Ne McMein, who lived in the hotel. She had a still in her bathroom.

When Oscar Wilde toured the United States on a lecture tour in the 1880s, he impressed Leadville, Colorado, miners with his ability to outdrink them. Their drink of choice? Gin, with dry vermouth.

OAKLAND COCKTAIL

4 parts vodka

2 parts dry vermouth

2 parts fresh orange juice

Combine all ingredients in a cocktail shaker with cracked ice and shake well. Strain into a chilled cocktail glass.

OCTOPUS'S GARDEN

6 parts gin

2 parts dry vermouth

Smoked baby octopus

Black olive

Combine liquid ingredients in a cocktail shaker with cracked ice and shake well. Strain into a chilled cocktail glass and garnish with octopus and olive.

OLD COUNTRY MARTINI

6 parts vodka

2 parts Madeira wine

2 parts cherry brandy

Orange twist

Combine liquid ingredients in a mixing glass with cracked ice and stir well. Strain into a chilled cocktail glass and garnish with orange twist.

OPAL MARTINI

6 parts gin
1 part triple sec
2 parts fresh orange juice
¼ teaspoon bar sugar

Combine all ingredients in a mixing glass with cracked ice and shake well. Strain into a chilled cocktail glass.

> "Everyone should believe in something. I believe I'll have another drink."
>
> —GROUCHO MARX

OPERA MARTINI ⇇

6 parts gin

2 parts Dubonnet blanc

1 part maraschino liqueur

Lemon twist

Combine liquid ingredients in a cocktail shaker with cracked ice and shake well. Strain into a chilled cocktail glass and garnish with lemon twist.

ORANGE MARTINI

6 parts vodka

1 part triple sec

1 dash orange bitters

Orange twist

Combine liquid ingredients in a cocktail shaker with cracked ice and shake well. Strain into a chilled cocktail glass and garnish with orange twist.

OSAKA DRY

6 parts vodka

1 part sake

Pickled plum

Combine liquid ingredients in a cocktail shaker with cracked ice and shake well. Strain into a chilled cocktail glass and garnish with pickled plum.

OYSTER MARTINI

6 parts vodka

1 part dry vermouth

Smoked oyster

Combine liquid ingredients in a cocktail shaker with cracked ice and shake well. Strain into a chilled cocktail glass and garnish with a smoked oyster on a toothpick.

PAISLEY MARTINI ➻

6 parts gin

1/2 teaspoon dry vermouth

1/2 teaspoon scotch

Cocktail olive

Combine liquid ingredients in a cocktail shaker with cracked ice and shake well. Strain into a chilled cocktail glass and garnish with olive.

"Happiness is a good martini, a good meal, a good cigar, and a good woman ... or a bad woman, depending on how much happiness you can stand."

—GEORGE BURNS

PALL MALL MARTINI

4 parts gin

1 part dry vermouth

1 part sweet vermouth

1 teaspoon white crème de menthe

1 dash orange bitters

Combine all ingredients in a mixing glass with ice cubes and stir well. Strain into a chilled cocktail glass.

PALM BEACH MARTINI →«

6 parts gin

1 teaspoon sweet vermouth

4 parts grapefruit juice

Combine all ingredients in a cocktail shaker with cracked ice and shake well. Strain into a chilled cocktail glass.

PARROTHEAD MARTINI

6 parts silver tequila

1 part triple sec

1 teaspoon fresh lime juice

Lime twist

Combine liquid ingredients in a cocktail shaker with cracked ice and shake well. Strain into a chilled cocktail glass and garnish with lime twist.

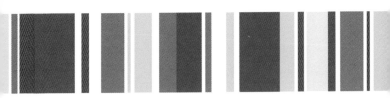

> "New York is the greatest city in the world for lunch. And when that first martini hits the liver like a silver bullet, there is a sigh of contentment that can be heard in Dubuque."
>
> —WILLIAM EMERSON, JR.

PARISIAN MARTINI ➻

6 parts gin

2 parts dry vermouth

1 part crème de cassis

Combine all ingredients in a cocktail shaker with cracked ice and shake well. Strain into a chilled cocktail glass.

PARK AVENUE MARTINI

6 parts gin

1 part sweet vermouth

1 part pineapple juice

Combine all ingredients in a cocktail shaker with cracked ice and shake well. Strain into a chilled cocktail glass.

PEACH BLOSSOM MARTINI ➻

6 parts peach vodka

1 part Dubonnet rouge

1 part maraschino liqueur

Fresh peach slice

Combine liquid ingredients in a cocktail shaker with cracked ice and shake well. Strain into a chilled cocktail glass and garnish with peach slice.

PEACHY MARTINI

6 parts strawberry-flavored vodka

2 parts peach brandy

Lemon twist

Combine liquid ingredients in a cocktail shaker with cracked ice and shake well. Strain into a chilled cocktail glass and garnish with lemon twist.

Dry Humor

A visitor to New York City walks into a midtown bar and orders a Manhattan. When it's placed before him, he notices that there's a sprig of parsley floating on top. "What is that thing in my Manhattan?" he asks the bartender. The bartender replies, without blinking, "That, sir, is Central Park."

PEAR PERFECTION

Granulated sugar

½ lime

1 shot vodka

2 shots pear nectar

Fresh pear slice

Moisten the outer rim of a chilled cocktail glass and dip in granulated sugar. Muddle the lime in a cocktail shaker then add cracked ice. Pour in vodka and pear nectar and shake well. Strain into the cocktail glass and garnish with pear slice.

PEGGY'S MARTINI

6 parts gin

1 part sweet vermouth

½ teaspoon Dubonnet rouge

½ teaspoon Pernod

Combine all ingredients in a mixing glass with cracked ice and stir well. Strain into a chilled cocktail glass.

PEPPERMINT MARTINI 🍸

6 parts pepper vodka

2 parts white crème de menthe

Fresh mint sprig

Combine liquid ingredients in a cocktail shaker with cracked ice and shake well. Strain into a chilled cocktail glass and garnish with mint sprig.

♈ | Did You Know?

Anecdotal history tells us that in 1608 Henry Hudson served gin to the Lenape Indians on an unnamed island. The Lenapes became very drunk, and when they recovered, named the island "Manhachtaniek" or "the island where we became intoxicated." Over the years, so the story goes, this name evolved into "Manhattan."

PERFECT MANHATTAN ➻

6 parts rye whiskey
1 part dry vermouth
1 part sweet vermouth
Maraschino cherry

Combine liquid ingredients in a cocktail shaker with cracked ice and shake well. Strain into a chilled cocktail glass and garnish with cherry.

PERFECT MARTINI

6 parts gin
1 part dry vermouth
1 part sweet vermouth
Cocktail olive

Combine liquid ingredients in a cocktail shaker with cracked ice and shake well. Strain into chilled cocktail glass and garnish with olive.

PERSEPHONE MARTINI

2 parts vodka

1 part pomegranate juice

Splash orange liqueur

Orange slice

Combine liquid ingredients in a cocktail shaker with ice. Shake well and strain into a chilled cocktail glass. Garnish with the orange slice.

PICADILLY MARTINI

6 parts gin

2 parts dry vermouth

½ teaspoon Pernod

1 dash grenadine

Combine all ingredients in a mixing glass with ice and stir well.
Strain into a chilled cocktail glass.

PINK GIN MARTINI

1 teaspoon Angostura bitters

8 parts gin

Pour bitters into a cocktail glass and swirl around until the inside
of the glass is completely coated with the bitters. Pour gin into the
glass. This drink should be served at room temperature.

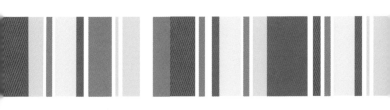

⏥ | Did You Know?

If you order a martini in England, you'll probably be served a glass of sweet vermouth. Be on the safe side, and order the British version of the martini—Pink Gin.

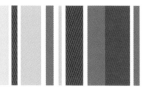

PLAZA MARTINI

2 parts gin

2 parts dry vermouth

2 parts sweet vermouth

Combine all ingredients in a cocktail shaker with cracked ice and shake well. Strain into a chilled cocktail glass.

POMPANO MARTINI

5 parts gin

1 part dry vermouth

2 parts fresh grapefruit juice

1 dash orange bitters

Combine all ingredients in a cocktail shaker with cracked ice and shake well. Strain into a chilled cocktail glass.

PRETTY MARTINI

4 parts vodka

1 part Grand Marnier

Orange twist

1 part amaretto

1 part dry vermouth

Combine liquid ingredients in a cocktail shaker with cracked ice and shake well. Strain into a chilled cocktail glass and garnish with orange twist.

PRINCE EDWARD MARTINI

6 parts gin

1 part Drambuie

Lemon twist

Combine liquid ingredients in a cocktail shaker with cracked ice and shake well. Strain into a chilled cocktail glass and garnish with lemon twist.

PRINCESS ELIZABETH MARTINI

6 parts sweet vermouth

1 part dry vermouth

2 teaspoons Benedictine

Combine all ingredients in a cocktail shaker with cracked ice and shake well. Strain into a chilled cocktail glass.

QUARTERDECK MARTINI

6 parts berry vodka

1 part maraschino liqueur

1 part grapefruit juice

Fresh mint sprig

Combine liquid ingredients in a mixing glass with cracked ice and stir well. Strain into a chilled cocktail glass and garnish with mint sprig.

"I've made it a rule never to drink by daylight and never to refuse a drink after dark."

—H.L. MENCKEN

A Drink before Its Time

The martini did not achieve widespread recognition in the United States until after Prohibition. It might have become more popular earlier, but the Volstead Act put an end to its ascension. During Prohibition, gin was the easiest of the hard liquors to bootleg, and rotgut—bathtub gin—became ubiquitous. It's no coincidence that sweet mixed drinks also became prevalent then. Drinkers wanted to mask the taste of the harsh homemade stuff. When prohibition ended, people could at last get fine, imported gin, and there was no need to dilute it. The martini, once again, was on its way to immortality.

QUEEN ELIZABETH MARTINI

6 parts gin

1 part dry vermouth

2 teaspoon Benedictine

Combine all ingredients in a cocktail shaker with cracked ice and shake well. Strain into a chilled cocktail glass.

RACQUET CLUB

6 parts gin

2 parts dry vermouth

3 to 5 dashes orange bitters

Combine all ingredients in a cocktail shaker with cracked ice and shake well. Strain into a chilled cocktail glass.

> "I know I'm not going to live forever, and neither are you, but until my furlough here on earth is revoked, I should like to elbow aside the established pieties and raise my martini glass in salute to the moral arts of pleasure."
>
> —BOB SHACOCHIS

RED DOG MARTINI ⚊

6 parts vodka

1 part ruby port

2 teaspoons fresh lime juice

1 teaspoon grenadine

Lime twist

Combine liquid ingredients in a cocktail shaker with cracked ice and shake well. Strain into a chilled cocktail glass and garnish with lime twist.

RENAISSANCE MARTINI ⚓

6 parts gin

1 part fino sherry

Grated nutmeg

Combine liquid ingredients in a cocktail shaker with cracked ice and shake well. Strain into a chilled cocktail glass and garnish with nutmeg.

RENDEZVOUS ♟

6 parts gin

2 parts cherry brandy

1 part Campari

Fresh cherries

Combine liquid ingredients in a cocktail shaker with cracked ice and shake well. Strain into a chilled cocktail glass and garnish with cherries.

RESOLUTION MARTINI

6 parts gin

2 parts apricot brandy

1 part fresh lemon juice

Combine ingredients in a cocktail shaker with cracked ice and shake well. Strain into a chilled cocktail glass.

ROADRUNNER MARTINI ←«

6 parts pepper-flavored vodka

1 part dry vermouth

1 part gold tequila

Jalapeño-stuffed olive

Combine liquid ingredients in a cocktail shaker with cracked ice and shake well. Strain into a chilled cocktail glass and garnish with jalapeño-stuffed olive.

ROLLS ROYCE

6 parts gin

2 parts dry vermouth

2 parts sweet vermouth

¼ teaspoon Benedictine

Combine all ingredients in a cocktail shaker with cracked ice and shake well. Strain into a chilled cocktail glass.

RUBY'S
RED GRAPEFRUIT MARTINI

Raw sugar

1½ ounces citrus-flavored or regular vodka

½ ounce triple sec

3 ounces red grapefruit juice

2 teaspoons raspberry liqueur

Grapefruit slices

Moisten the rim of a chilled cocktail glass and dip in raw sugar. Combine the liquid ingredients in a cocktail shaker with cracked ice and shake well. Strain into the cocktail glass and slowly pour in the raspberry liqueur so that it comes to rest on the bottom of the glass. Garnish with grapefruit slices.

RUM MARTINI ✈

6 parts light rum

1 part dry vermouth

1 dash orange bitters

Almond-stuffed olive

Combine liquid ingredients in a cocktail shaker with cracked ice and shake well. Strain into a chilled cocktail glass and garnish with almond-stuffed olive.

RUSSIAN MARTINI

4 parts vodka

4 parts gin

1 part white chocolate liqueur

Combine all ingredients in a cocktail shaker with cracked ice and shake well. Strain into a chilled cocktail glass.

RUSSIAN ROSE

6 parts strawberry-flavored vodka

1 part dry vermouth

1 part grenadine

1 dash orange bitters

Combine all ingredients in a mixing glass with cracked ice and stir well. Strain into a chilled cocktail glass.

SAKETINI ⤚

6 parts gin

1 part sake

Lemon twist wrapped with

Pickled ginger

Combine liquid ingredients in a cocktail shaker with cracked ice and shake well. Strain into a chilled cocktail glass and garnish with lemon twist.

SECRET MARTINI

6 parts gin

2 parts Lillet blanc

2 dashes Angostura bitters

Cocktail olive

Combine liquid ingredients in a mixing glass with cracked ice and stir well. Strain into a chilled cocktail glass and garnish with olive.

SEVENTH HEAVEN ⚓

6 parts gin

1 part maraschino liqueur

1 part grapefruit juice

Fresh mint sprig

Combine liquid ingredients in a mixing glass with cracked ice and stir well. Strain into a chilled cocktail glass and garnish with mint sprig.

[The martini is] "the only American invention as perfect as a sonnet."

—H.L. MENCKEN

SEXY DEVIL

4 parts vodka

2 parts cranberry vodka

1 part dry vermouth

Lemon peel

Fresh strawberry

Combine liquid ingredients in a cocktail shaker with cracked ice and shake well. Strain into a chilled cocktail glass and garnish with lemon peel and strawberry.

Did You Know?

The debonair erstwhile detective Nick Charles shakes all of his cocktails. In the classic 1934 film *The Thin Man,* he advises, "Always have rhythm in your shaking. Now a Manhattan you shake to fox-trot time, a Bronx to two-step time, a dry martini you always shake to waltz time."

SHRIMPTINI

6 parts gin or vodka

2 parts dry vermouth

Dash of Tabasco

Large cooked shrimp

Combine liquid ingredients in a cocktail shaker with cracked ice and shake well. Strain into a chilled cocktail glass and garnish with cooked shrimp.

SILVER STREAK

6 parts gin

3 parts Jagermeister

Lemon twist

Combine liquid ingredients in a mixing glass with cracked ice and stir well. Strain into a chilled cocktail glass and garnish with lemon twist.

> "The three-martini lunch is the epitome of American efficiency. Where else can you get an earful, a bellyful, and a snootful at the same time?"
>
> —GERALD FORD

SLOE GIN MARTINI

6 parts sloe gin

2 parts dry vermouth

3 to 5 dashes Angostura bitters

Lemon twist

Combine liquid ingredients in a cocktail shaker with cracked ice and shake well. Strain into a chilled cocktail glass and garnish with lemon twist.

SMOKESTACK LIGHTNING

1 shot premium whiskey

6 parts vodka

1 part vermouth

Lemon zest cut into lightning bolt shape

Coat a chilled cocktail glass with a shot of whiskey and discard (or drink!) the excess. Combine the vodka and vermouth in a cocktail shaker with cracked ice and stir or shake well. Strain into prepared cocktail glass. Garnish with lemon zest lightning bolt.

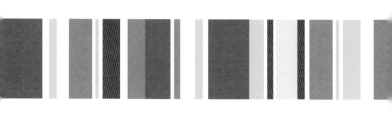

SMOKY MARTINI

6 parts gin

1 part dry vermouth

1 teaspoon scotch

Lemon twist

Combine liquid ingredients in a mixing glass with cracked ice and stir well. Strain into a chilled cocktail glass and garnish with lemon twist.

SOUTHERN MARTINI

6 parts gin

1 part triple sec

3 to 5 dashes orange bitters

Lemon twist

Combine liquid ingredients in a mixing glass with cracked ice and stir well. Strain into a chilled cocktail glass and garnish with lemon twist.

SOUR APPLE MARTINI

2 ounces citrus-flavored vodka

½ ounce sour apple schnapps

½ ounce orange liqueur

¾ ounce fresh lemon juice

Thin green apple slice

Combine liquid ingredients in a cocktail shaker with cracked ice and shake well. Strain into a chilled cocktail glass and garnish with apple slice.

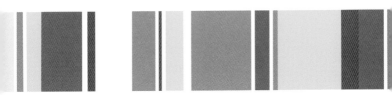

SOUR CHERRY SPARKLETINI

1 ounce cherry-flavored vodka

1 ounce sweet-tart cherry schnapps

1 splash lemon-lime soda

Fresh cherry on a stem

Combine liquid ingredients in a cocktail shaker with cracked ice and shake well. Drop the cherry into a chilled cocktail glass and strain the martini over it.

SOVIET MARTINI

6 parts ashberry-flavored or currant vodka

1 part dry vermouth

1 part fino sherry

Lemon twist

Combine liquid ingredients in a mixing glass with cracked ice and stir well. Strain into a chilled cocktail glass and garnish with lemon twist.

> ## "All you need is love, love or, failing that, alcohol.
> —WENDY COPE, ENGLISH POET

SPICE IT UP CINNAMON MARTINI

1 part vodka

Dash cinnamon schnapps (regular or extra hot)

Red Hots candies

Place vodka in a cocktail shaker with ice and shake well. Strain vodka into a chilled cocktail glass and add cinnamon schnapps. Garnish with Red Hots.

NOTE: FOR A FESTIVE SPARKLING CINNAMON MARTINI, USE GOLDSCHLAGER CINNAMON SCHNAPPS AND OMIT THE RED HOTS.

SPICED TREAT MARTINI

6 parts cinnamon vodka

1 part chocolate liqueur

1 part coffee liqueur

Chocolate cocktail straw

Combine liquid ingredients in a mixing glass with cracked ice and stir well. Strain into a chilled cocktail glass and garnish with chocolate straw.

 Did You Know?

In one musical number of the 1949 Broadway production of *Gentlemen Prefer Blondes*, Miles White's award-winning costumes featured two martinis per showgirl—one over each breast—with nipples doing double duty as olives.

SPRINGTIME MARTINI

6 parts buffalo grass vodka
2 parts Lillet blanc
Miniature pickled asparagus spear

Combine liquid ingredients in a cocktail shaker with cracked ice and shake well. Strain into a chilled cocktail glass and garnish with asparagus spear.

> "Before I start to write, I always treat myself to a nice dry martini. Just one, to give me the courage to get started. After that, I am on my own."
>
> —E.B. WHITE

STATEN ISLAND COCKTAIL

6 parts coffee vodka

1 part dry vermouth

2 parts fresh lime juice

Maraschino cherry

Combine liquid ingredients in a cocktail shaker with cracked ice and shake well. Strain into a chilled cocktail glass and garnish with cherry.

STRAWBERRY BLONDE ←

6 parts strawberry vodka

2 parts Lillet blanc

Fresh strawberry

Combine liquid ingredients in a cocktail shaker with cracked ice and shake well. Strain into a chilled cocktail glass and garnish with fresh strawberry.

ST. PETERSBURG

6 parts vodka

3 to 5 dashes orange bitters

Orange peel

Combine liquid ingredients in a cocktail shaker with cracked ice and shake well. Strain into a chilled cocktail glass and garnish with orange peel.

SUMMER BREEZE

6 parts citrus vodka

2 parts melon liqueur

1 part dry vermouth

¼ teaspoon fresh lemon juice

Melon ball

Combine liquid ingredients in a mixing glass with ice cubes and stir well. Strain into a chilled cocktail glass and garnish with melon ball.

SWEET AND SPICY MARTINI ◂◂

6 parts cinnamon vodka

1 part sweet vermouth

1 part orange liqueur

Cinnamon stick

Combine liquid ingredients in a cocktail shaker with cracked ice and shake well. Strain into a chilled cocktail glass and garnish with cinnamon stick.

SWEET BLOSSOM

¾ ounce apple brandy

¾ ounce sweet vermouth

2 teaspoons apricot brandy

1½ teaspoons fresh lemon juice

Apple blossom (or other delicate flower)

Combine liquid ingredients in a cocktail shaker with cracked ice and shake well. Strain into a chilled cocktail glass and garnish with apple blossom.

SWEET MARTINI ➳

6 parts gin

2 parts sweet vermouth

1 dash orange bitters

Lime twist

Combine liquid ingredients in a mixing glass with cracked ice and stir well. Strain into a chilled cocktail glass and garnish with lime twist.

SWEET TARTINI

2 ounces lemon- or orange-flavored vodka

½ ounce fresh lemon juice

¼ ounce fresh pomegranate juice

1 ounce simple syrup (see page 22)

Lemon twist

Combine liquid ingredients in a cocktail shaker with cracked iced. Shake well and strain into a chilled cocktail glass. Garnish with lemon twist.

SWEETIE MARTINI

6 parts gin

1 part dry vermouth

1 part sweet vermouth

Lemon twist

Combine liquid ingredients in a cocktail shaker with cracked ice and shake well. Strain into a chilled cocktail glass and garnish with lemon twist.

TEQUINI

6 parts silver tequila

1 part dry vermouth

1 dash orange bitters

Lemon twist (see note)

Combine liquid ingredients in a cocktail shaker with cracked ice and shake well. Strain into a chilled cocktail glass and garnish with lemon twist.

NOTE: ENHANCE THIS DRINK BY RUBBING THE LEMON TWIST OVER THE RIM OF THE GLASS.

THIRD DEGREE MARTINI ➻

6 parts gin

2 parts dry vermouth

1 part Pernod

Star anise

Combine liquid ingredients in a cocktail shaker with cracked ice and shake well. Strain into a chilled cocktail glass and garnish with star anise.

THREE STRIPES

4 parts gin

2 parts dry vermouth

2 parts fresh orange juice

Combine all ingredients in a cocktail shaker with cracked ice and shake well. Strain into a chilled cocktail glass.

Fringe Benefits

Raymond Chandler, the great American mystery novelist, really didn't want to write the screenplay for the film of *The Blue Dahlia*, so he struck a deal with his producer, John Houseman. He agreed to write the script only if it was written into his contract that he could write it while drunk. The contract also had to include the following: Paramount would provide limousines, secretaries, and nurses for Chandler twenty-four hours a day, a doctor would be on call to administer vitamin shots since Chandler never ate when he was drinking, and there would be a direct phone line from his house to the studio. The studio would also take the Chandlers' maid shopping. Houseman agreed to this over lunch with Chandler, at which time Chandler had three double martinis and three stingers. He went straight to work after lunch and finished the screenplay in about two weeks.

TOOTSIE ROLL MARTINI

6 parts vodka

1 part chocolate liqueur

1 part Grand Marnier

Orange twist

Combine liquid ingredients in a cocktail shaker with cracked ice and shake well. Strain into a chilled cocktail glass and garnish with orange twist.

TOVARISCH ⇥

6 parts vodka

2 parts kümmel

2 parts fresh lime juice

Black olive

Combine liquid ingredients in a cocktail shaker with cracked ice and shake well. Strain into a chilled cocktail glass and garnish with black olive.

TRUFFLE MARTINI

6 parts strawberry vodka

1 part Grand Marnier

1 part chocolate liqueur

Orange twist

Combine liquid ingredients in a cocktail shaker with cracked ice and shake well. Strain into a chilled cocktail glass and garnish with orange twist.

TURF MARTINI

4 parts gin

2 parts dry vermouth

1 part Pernod

1 part fresh lemon juice

3 to 5 dashes Angostura bitters

Almond-stuffed olive

Combine liquid ingredients in a cocktail shaker with cracked ice and shake well. Strain into a chilled cocktail glass and garnish with almond-stuffed olive.

TUXEDO

4 parts vodka

3 parts dry vermouth

½ teaspoon maraschino liqueur

3 to 5 dashes orange bitters

Lemon twist

Combine liquid ingredients in a cocktail shaker with cracked ice and shake well. Strain into a chilled cocktail glass and garnish with lemon twist.

ULANDA

4 parts gin

2 parts triple sec

1 tablespoon Pernod

Combine all ingredients in a mixing glass with cracked ice and stir well. Strain into a chilled cocktail glass.

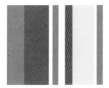

"Let schoolmasters puzzle their brains with grammar and nonsense and learning; good liquor, I stoutly maintain, gives genius better discerning."

—OLIVER GOLDSMITH

UNBRIDLED PASSIONFRUIT MARTINI

1½ ounces Alize
½ ounce vodka
Lime twist

Combine the liquid ingredients in a cocktail shaker with cracked ice and shake well. Strain into a chilled cocktail glass and garnish with lime twist.

Famous Martini Drinkers

Robert Benchley

Humphrey Bogart

James Bond

Carrie Bradshaw

Luis Buñuel

Herb Caen

Raymond Chandler

Winston Churchill

William Faulkner

W.C. Fields

F. Scott and Zelda Fitzgerald

Gerald Ford

Robert Frost

Jackie Gleason

Ernest Hemingway

John F. Kennedy

Dorothy Lewis (Sinclair Lewis' wife)

W. Somerset Maugham

H.L. Mencken

Richard Nixon

Dorothy Parker

Franklin Delano Roosevelt

Mae West

E.B. White

Billy Wilder

P.G. Wodehouse

Alexander Woollcott

VALENCIA MARTINI ⚓

6 parts gin
2 parts amontillado sherry
Olive

Combine liquid ingredients in a mixing glass with cracked ice and stir well. Strain into a chilled cocktail glass and garnish with olive.

Did You Know?

Ian Fleming's James Bond not only drank vodka martinis, he also drank champagne, sherry, scotch—whatever the occasion called for. But the cinematic James Bond was a hard-core vodka martini drinker, largely because Smirnoff bought the product placement rights. The popularity of the Bond films helped make the vodka martini the most popular drink of the 1960s.

VANILLA TWIST ❦

6 parts vanilla vodka
1 part Cointreau
1 part dry vermouth
Vanilla bean

Combine liquid ingredients in a cocktail shaker with cracked ice and shake well. Strain into a chilled cocktail glass and garnish with vanilla bean.

Hangover Helpers

The martinis went down smoothly last night, but now those silver bullets feel like they're lodged in your brain. You got yourself into this mess—how do you get yourself out? As you probably know, there are no surefire hangover cures, but there are some things you can try to ease the pain:

- •DRINK, DRINK, DRINK. No, not more martinis. Drink lots of water, rehydrating sports drinks (such as Gatorade), or mild juice (avoid orange juice and grapefruit, which can aggravate your already sensitive stomach).

- •TAKE AN ANTACID. Some swear by the effervescent ones— yes, "Plop, plop, fizz, fizz."—because they not only soothe the beast in the belly, but also ease pounding headaches.

- •SLEEP IT OFF. You've just subjected your body to a wild ride, albeit a fun one. Take it easy and try to take a cat nap or two if you can. And go to bed early for heaven's sake!

- •EAT A RAW EGG. Down a pot of strong, black coffee; or take the hair of the dog (i.e., drink more booze). Do you think we're nuts?! We don't consider these good options unless you want to feel worse. But if any of these are your method of choice, more power to you. Just don't tell anyone you read it here.

WAIKIKI MARTINI

6 parts pineapple vodka

1 part dry vermouth

1 part Lillet blanc

Pineapple wedge

Combine liquid ingredients in a cocktail shaker with cracked ice and shake well. Strain into a chilled cocktail glass and garnish with pineapple wedge.

WARSAW MARTINI

4 parts potato vodka

1 part dry vermouth

1 part blackberry brandy

1 tablespoon fresh lemon juice

Combine all ingredients in a cocktail shaker with cracked ice and shake well. Strain into a chilled cocktail glass.

WEMBLY MARTINI

6 parts gin

1 part dry vermouth

1 teaspoon apricot brandy

1 teaspoon Calvados

Lemon twist

Combine liquid ingredients in a cocktail shaker with cracked ice and shake well. Strain into a chilled cocktail glass and garnish with lemon twist.

WHAT IS THAT MARTINI?

6 parts vodka

1 part Sambuca

Licorice twist

3 coffee beans

Combine liquid ingredients in a mixing glass with cracked ice and stir well. Strain into a chilled cocktail glass and garnish with licorice twist and coffee beans.

WISE ELDERFLOWER MARTINI

2 ounces gin

1 ounce fresh lime juice

½ ounce elderflower cordial

Dash of simple syrup (see page 22)

Dash of orange bitters

Lime or orange twist

Combine liquid ingredients in a cocktail shaker with cracked ice and stir until shaker becomes icy cold. Strain into a chilled cocktail glass and garnish with lime or orange twist.

WOO WOO MARTINI

6 parts cranberry vodka

1 part peach schnapps

Lemon twist

Combine liquid ingredients in a cocktail shaker with cracked ice and shake well. Strain into a chilled cocktail glass and garnish with lemon twist.

XENA MARTINI

5 parts honey-flavored vodka

1 part buffalo grass vodka

1 teaspoon Lillet blanc

Pickled asparagus spear

Combine liquid ingredients in a cocktail shaker with cracked ice and shake well. Strain into a chilled cocktail glass and garnish with asparagus spear.

YES, WE HAVE NO BANANAS

1 ounce Kahlua

1 ounce vodka

½ ounce banana liqueur

Banana slices

Combine liquid ingredients in a cocktail shaker with cracked ice. Shake well and strain into a chilled cocktail glass. Garnish with banana slices.

ZIPPY MARTINI

6 parts vodka

1 part dry vermouth

3 to 4 dashes Tabasco sauce

Pickled jalapeño pepper slice

Combine liquid ingredients in a cocktail shaker with cracked ice and shake well. Strain into a chilled cocktail glass and garnish with pickled jalapeño slice.

INDEX

RECIPES ➜

Bold indicates illustration

INDEX

INGREDIENTS ➻ ||||| | ||| || |

V

vermouth, 23, 50; brands, 23; dry, 34, 40, 41, 42, 44, 47, 49, 50, 52, 52, 54, 58, 61, 62, 65, 71, 73, 74, 76, 78, 79, 80, 82, 83, 84, 89, 92, 93, 95, 96, 97, 98, 99, 100, 103, 107, 108, 111, 112, 113, 115, 116, 118, 119, 121, 124, 127, 132, 135, 136, 140, 142, 144, 145, 146, 151, 152, 153, 155, 156, 158, 159, 160, 165, 167, 168, 170, 174, 177, 179, 180, 182; sweet, 12, 40, 42, 43, 47, 78, 86, 92, 93, 95, 97, 100, 103, 107, 108, 115, 116, 118, 119, 122, 124, 135, 136, 139, 140, 143, 144, 145, 151, 167, 168

vodka, 19-21, 39, 40, 42, 43, 48, 49, 55, 57, 58, 61, 68, 72, 74, 75, 76, 80, 82, 83, 84, 86, 89, 92, 93, 99, 103, 107, 111, 113, 114, 119, 126, 127, 131, 132, 138, 141, 144, 147, 151, 153, 155, 156, 158, 161, 165, 172, 174, 175, 180, 182; ashberry, 160; berry, 93, 145; brands, 20; buffalo grass, 84, 96, 100, 162, 182; cherry, 160; chocolate, 57; chocolate-orange, 57; cinnamon, 161, 167; citrus, 72, 76, 90, 108, 151, 167; coffee, 56, 65, 73, 79, 82, 98, 121, 165; cranberry, 155, 181; currant, 42, 44, 101, 121, 125, 160; flavored, 21; honey, 66, 75, 182; lemon, 64, 66, 111, 168; orange, 57, 65, 105, 168; peach, 136; pepper, 54, 96, 97, 139, 151; pineapple, 179; potato, 180; raspberry, 81; strawberry, 42, 138, 153, 165, 172; vanilla, 41, 44, 79, 82, 106, 114, 124, 125, 177

W

water, 31

West, Mae, 175

whiskey, 21, 158; Irish, 100

White, E. B., 26, 165, 175

White, Miles, 161

Wilde, Oscar, 127

Wilder, Billy, 43, 175

wine, cherry, 57; Madeira, 124, 127; port, 71, 147; red, 55, 101; sparkling, 56, 81; white, 118

Wodehouse, P. G., 175

Woollcott, Alexander, 43, 175

Photo credits

T = top
B = bottom
L = left
R = right

Photos by Zeva Oelbaum, except for:
Pages 2-3: Michal Kram/istockphoto
6: Sandra O'Claire/istockphoto
10: Sandra O'Claire/istockphoto
13T: Rick Rhay/istockphoto
13B: Dave Waisglass/istockphoto
14: Mark Aplet/istockphoto
18: Alex Bramwell/istockphoto
20: Ivan Mateev/istockphoto
22T: Pawel Janowski/istockphoto
22B: Gergely Cziva/istockphoto
24L: Hugo Chang/istockphoto
24R: istockphoto
25B: Sarit Saliman/istockphoto
29: Paul Kooi/istockphoto
30T: Rick Rhay/istockphoto
30L: John Long/istockphoto
30R: Wolfgang Major/istockphoto
31T: Lisa McDonald/istockphoto
31B: Ruslan Gil Manshin/istockphoto
32-33: Alex Bramwell/istockphoto
35T: Kelly Cline/istockphoto
35B: Alex Bramwell/istockphoto
36-37: Alex Bramwell/istockphoto
41: Justin Griffith/istockphoto
60-61: Leah-Anne Thompson/istockphoto
69: Rebecca Picard/istockphoto
74: Ivan Mateev/istockphoto
87: Chris Bence/istockphoto
91: Kasia Beil/istockphoto
93: Stefan Klein/istockphoto
97: Odelia Cohen/istockphoto
104-105: Marcy Smith/istockphoto
110: Cara Purdy/istockphoto
112: Alex Bramwell/istockphoto
117: Rebecca Ellis/istockphoto
143: Jennifer Sheets/istockphoto
147: Alex Bramwell/istockphoto
183: Gary Allard/istockphoto